Explorers Who Made It...
or died trying

Frieda Wishinsky

cover by **Eric Olson**
illustrations by **Bill Dickson**

Scholastic Canada Ltd.
Toronto New York London Auckland Sydney
Mexico City New Delhi Hong Kong Buenos Aires

To Heather and Tamara, who made exploring a joy.

Scholastic Canada Ltd.
604 King Street West, Toronto, Ontario M5V 1E1, Canada

Scholastic Inc.
557 Broadway, New York, NY 10012, USA

Scholastic Australia Pty Limited
PO Box 579, Gosford, NSW 2250, Australia

Scholastic New Zealand Limited
Private Bag 94407, Botany, Manukau 2163, New Zealand

Scholastic Children's Books
Euston House, 24 Eversholt Street, London NW1 1DB, UK

Library and Archives Canada Cataloguing in Publication
Wishinsky, Frieda
Explorers who made it-- or died trying / Frieda Wishinsky ; Bill Dickson,
illustrator.
Includes index.
ISBN 978-1-4431-0010-6
1. Explorers--Biography--Juvenile literature. 2. Discoveries in
geography--History--Juvenile literature. I. Dickson, Bill II. Title.
G200.W57 2011   j910.92'2   C2011-901359-2

6 5 4 3 2 1   Printed in Canada 121   11 12 13 14 15 16

MIX
Paper from
responsible sources
FSC® C004071
www.fsc.org

Table of Contents

Why Explorers Fascinate Me

Okay, I admit it. I wouldn't climb a mountain just because it was there, or sail on unknown seas if monsters lurked, or freeze my toes off just to plant a flag on a slab of ice at the bottom or top of the world. But people who did just that fascinate me. Why did they risk everything? Why did they brave storms, starvation and sickness? What was it about their times, goals and temperaments that made these explorers set out for the unknown? What did they hope to discover? What did they actually find, and how did they feel about the unexpected results of their journeys? Why did they continue to explore after almost dying while trying? Were they fearless, foolish or both?

Here are the stories of intrepid explorers who risked everything to conquer the unknown.

A few things to note before we start:

- *Circa* is Latin for "approximately." It's used when historians are not sure of a date.
- The terms "Indies," "East Indies," "The East" and "Spice Islands" have all been used by explorers to describe the Asian lands where spices grow. Those lands are now called Indonesia, Southeast Asia and India.

Watch Out!
Here Come the Vikings!

Erik The Red (*circa* 950–1003)
and Leif Eriksson (*circa* 980–1020)

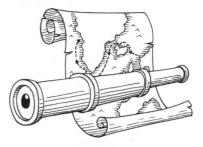

 What do you do if you're a Viking
and your land is hard to farm?

1. Complain a lot.
2. Experiment with new ways to grow food.
3. Sail off to find better land.
4. Sail off to steal other people's better land.

If you picked answers 3 or 4, you're right. The
Vikings, a fierce people who lived in a tough climate
and on rocky, hard-to-farm land, sailed off to find
better land and more food. Sometimes they traded
or bartered, but often they swooped in and stole in
sudden, unexpected and brutal raids.

If this makes the Vikings sound terrifying and
ruthless, that's because they were. But they had good
qualities too. They were amazing sailors. They played

by a set of rules and gave women more rights than most societies did at the time. They discovered land (North America) that was new to Europeans. True, the Vikings didn't stay long, but they did check North America out.

Why did the Vikings sail where no other European had ventured before? What happened when they arrived? And why did they leave their newly discovered land, never to return? It's a story that begins with a murderer called Erik the Red.

Who Was Erik the Red?

Erik's full name was Erik Thorvaldsson, but his flaming red hair and beard earned him the nickname "Erik the Red." Erik lived in what is now Norway. He was a lot like his father, Thorvald. They were both tough guys who always got into fights and sometimes killed people in the scuffles.

One day Erik and Thorvald killed a man in a dispute. Before the man's angry relatives could take revenge, father and son sailed off to safety in Iceland. There Erik married a woman called Thorhild and settled down.

Now that he was a husband and landowner, did Erik change his murderous ways? No! Not Erik. He was soon embroiled in another dispute and killed another Viking. What now? Run again? Absolutely!

Erik hightailed it to Breidha Fjord on the northwest coast of Iceland. By this time, you'd think he would have had enough of killing and moving, but Erik could never resist a juicy feud. He killed another guy in a fight, and this time the Viking council ordered him out of Iceland, banishing him for three years.

I'll Take That Island!

What now?

In the spring of 981, Erik sailed off on his 30-metre (100-foot) long ship with a small crew. Eight hundred kilometres (500 miles) westward they sighted land. But what they'd sighted wasn't a tiny sliver of land. It was a gigantic island!

And the place didn't look bad. Erik circumnavigated it and found that although the interior was full of glaciers, the coast was green and dotted with fjords and hills like his native Norway. There were herds of reindeer and caribou to hunt. Walruses and seals lounged on rocks. Birds filled the sky. There was abundant food just waiting for a hungry Viking.

Would you . . .

like being called

- Ivar the Boneless?
- Harald Bluetooth?
- Eyiolf the Foul?
- Erik Bloodax?
- Svein Forkbeard?

You might not. But those were real Viking names.

But it wasn't enough. Although Erik was hot-tempered, he wasn't a loner. He wanted people to talk to, share a meal with and have a few laughs with over a roaring fire. He needed to attract settlers to his new land.

But how do you make people want to live in an unknown land? How do you encourage them to leave everyone and everything familiar behind? How do you make a place sound so beautiful, so inviting that people will clamour to move?

Come to Greenland!
It's a Great Place to Live!

There was only one thing to do — advertise! And if you start with a catchy name, you're halfway there. So Erik decided to call his new land Greenland. After all, "green" suggested lush pastures, abundant crops and lots of food. And times were tough in Iceland. There was a famine, and good farming land was scarce.

After Erik's three years of banishment were over, he returned to Iceland to recruit settlers for Greenland. In no time, he gathered 25 shiploads of people, animals and goods, and in the year 986 they sailed

COME TO SUNNY GREENLAND
FREE SWORDS FOR THE KIDDIES!

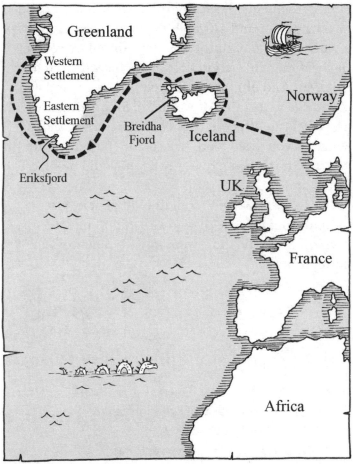

Norway to Greenland

off. But a storm kicked up and the flotilla of ships was hammered. Some turned back. Others kept on sailing. Only 14 ships reached Greenland.

When they finally arrived, the new settlers were tired and bedraggled, yet determined. They began to build settlements. The captain of each ship picked a favourite fjord and moved his family there. Erik picked a place he called Eriksfjord (after himself, of course). He lived there like a *jarl* (lord) with his wife and four children. And although like Iceland, Greenland wasn't conducive to farming, it was good for grazing animals and catching fish. You could even survive in the winter, if you dried food, like cod, by hanging it up till it turned hard as a plank. Then you could break off pieces and chew.

As he grew older, Erik didn't kill people, just animals and fish. He died in Greenland in 1003 from an epidemic that swept in with a new group of immigrants.

POP

QUIZ Why was Leif Eriksson called "Leif the Lucky"?

1. He always won at arm wrestling.
2. He always won at Go Fish.
3. He saved some shipwrecked sailors from a trading ship, and they rewarded him.

If you picked answer number 3, you're right. Leif was also lucky that he didn't inherit his father's hot temper and nasty habit of getting into fights. Leif was level-headed and fair-minded. What Leif *did* inherit, though, was an itch to explore.

Who was Leif Eriksson?

Leif was born in Iceland around 980 but grew up in Greenland. He was cared for by an educated German slave named Thyrker, who taught him how to read and write runes, a Viking script, and to speak Irish and Russian.

When he was 24, Leif took off for Norway to trade. Greenland was low on timber, and Norway was rich in wood, so they often traded.

Leif decided to take a route to Norway that no one else had tried. On the way, he was blown off course by a storm. Fortunately he found a safe place to stay for the winter, and he fell in love with a nice local girl. (Yes! Lucky Leif again!)

When he finally reached Norway and met King Olaf, the king was impressed with his bravery and navigational skills. The king convinced Leif to become a Christian and asked him to spread the word about the new faith.

An Itch to Explore

Leif returned to Greenland and tried to persuade other Vikings to become Christians. (His mother said she would convert. His father, Erik the Red, said, "No way.") He also decided he wasn't ready to settle down and farm but wanted to explore instead. When

he heard about some lands that the Viking Bjarni
Herjolfsson had passed while blown off course, he
knew that he had to see those lands. He'd find a crew
and a ship and sail off.

Leif asked his father to join him on the journey,
but Erik refused. Erik felt he was too old and too sick
to travel, so Leif bought Bjarni's ship, gathered a crew
(including his old tutor Thyrker) and they took off for
the unknown.

The first place they sighted was glacier-covered
and rocky, and Leif was not impressed. He called it
Helluland, which means "land of flat stones." (It's
called Baffin Island today.)

Leif then sailed south and came upon a heavily
forested land that looked better than Helluland but not
good enough for more than a quick stopover. Leif called
that place Markland (it's now Labrador), and sailed on.

Finally they landed at a place with rivers teeming with salmon and vines dripping with fruit. It looked good and it smelled good and the days were longer than in Greenland. (Now we know it as the northeastern tip of Newfoundland.) Leif named the place Vinland, and he and his crew decided to stay for the winter. When summer came they returned to Greenland.

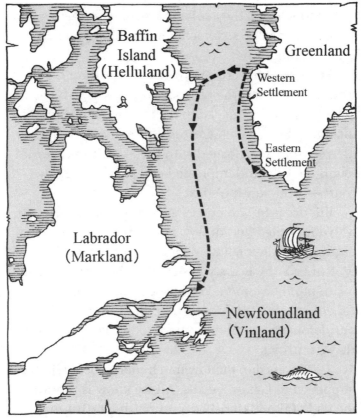

Greenland to Vinland

Stuck at Home

Soon after, Erik the Red died and Leif became head of the family. He was now in charge of running the farm and making decisions for his clan, so he couldn't leave home to explore. Instead he loaned his ship to his brother Thorvald to sail to Vinland.

Thorvald was not as lucky as Leif. When he and his crew anchored in Vinland, they encountered unfriendly locals they called Skraelings. After a skirmish, one of the Skraelings shot Thorvald with an arrow, killing him.

The rest of his crew returned to Greenland, but Vinland still drew the Eriksson family. Some other family members decided to try their luck in Vinland, including Erik's sister, Freydis. But not long after they arrived, they too clashed with the Skraelings. Freydis fought fiercely and impressed everyone with her courage and fighting spirit.

But according to one version of the Sagas, Freydis, who'd inherited her father's hot temper, soon began arguing with her fellow Vikings over property. In typical Erik-the-Red style, she killed her adversaries, including the women. When she returned to Greenland, she tried to hush up the rumours of her murderous behaviour, but her brother Leif found out. He was furious.

The Sagas don't tell us much more about what happened to Leif or Freydis. All we know is that was the end of the Vikings' adventures in North America. They never returned to Vinland or to any other place

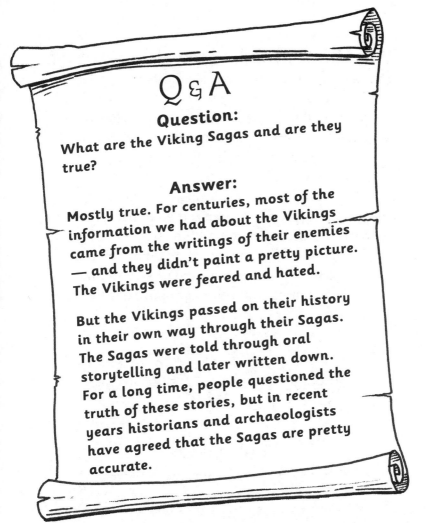

Q & A

Question:

What are the Viking Sagas and are they true?

Answer:

Mostly true. For centuries, most of the information we had about the Vikings came from the writings of their enemies — and they didn't paint a pretty picture. The Vikings were feared and hated.

But the Vikings passed on their history in their own way through their Sagas. The Sagas were told through oral storytelling and later written down. For a long time, people questioned the truth of these stories, but in recent years historians and archaeologists have agreed that the Sagas are pretty accurate.

on the North American continent. Were they afraid of fighting the rambunctious Skraelings? Were they too busy eking out a living in Greenland? Were they happy to just continue raiding and looting in Europe? Historians have come up with many theories, but no definite answers.

What Do We Think of the Vikings Today?

In the early 1960s, two archaeologists and writers made a startling discovery in L'Anse aux Meadows in Newfoundland. They found physical evidence of Viking settlements. That proved it! Leif Eriksson and his Viking crew were the first Europeans to land in North America.

The Vikings also left a strong mark on Europe. They not only plundered, but settled in new places and married the locals. There's Viking ancestry not just in Iceland, Norway and Sweden, but in many other countries. So, if you ever have the urge to sail the seas or to eat dried cod, you might have a little bit of Viking blood running through your veins.

Report Card

Erik the Red

Daring.. *A*

Persistence.. *A*

Getting Along with Others................................... *D-*

Leif Eriksson

Daring.. *A*

Persistence .... *B+*

Getting Along with Others.................................... *A*

Hey, Dad!
I Wanna Go to China!

Marco Polo (*circa* 1254–1324)

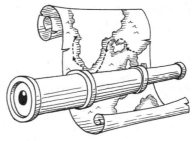

What do you say to your father when he's been away for nine years?

1. Who are you?
2. Where were you?
3. Did you bring me anything?
4. Can I come with you next time?

If you picked all four answers, you're probably right — although there's no record that young Marco Polo actually asked these questions when his father came back from years in the East with his brother, Marco's uncle. It just makes sense that he would. Wouldn't you?

If it wasn't for a book written by Marco Polo in 1298 in a Genoese jail, we wouldn't know anything about his *own* fantastic adventures in the East. Although many people scoffed at the strange and even bizarre tales he told in *The Description of the World* (also called *The Travels of Marco Polo* or *Il Milione*), and some people even called Marco a liar, his book became a bestseller. Over the centuries it inspired other explorers, like Christopher Columbus, to venture into the unknown.

So who *was* this great traveller and teller of tales? Are his stories true or the outpourings of a vivid imagination?

Who Was Marco Polo?

The story of Marco Polo's fabulous journey starts in 1269, when his father Niccolo and his uncle Maffeo showed up in Venice, Italy, after nine years of trading in the East. No one had heard from the two men in years. That wasn't surprising. There was no way to send mail in Europe in the 13th century.

No one would have been surprised, either, if they never came back. In those days travelling was treacherous. You could fall ill on the road without a doctor or medicine. You could tumble off a jagged mountain or lose your way (and maybe your mind) in an arid, endless desert. You could die at the hand of bandits or in a storm. There were so many ways to run into trouble on the road, it was a wonder anyone came back.

Most people thought that the Polo brothers were never returning to Venice. Imagine everyone's shock when they appeared. And imagine Marco's feelings. He hardly knew his father or uncle. He was only six years old when they left. His mother had died soon after, and his aunt and uncle had brought him up.

But, of course, the family was thrilled when the men returned, and they threw them a big "welcome home" party. Everyone was keen to hear about the traders' adventures in exotic Constantinople (then the capital of the Latin Empire), and with the great and powerful Mongol Emperor, Kublai Khan, in China. They weren't disappointed. The two men told fantastic tales. Some were so fantastic it was hard to believe they were true.

Marco couldn't get enough of the stories and, two years later in 1271, when his father and uncle were ready to set off again, he begged to join them. Niccolo and Maffeo agreed.

The Polos were happy to hit the road again and delighted to take the enthusiastic and clever Marco. They wanted to leave soon. They were bored hanging around Venice, working as everyday merchants. They longed to return to the danger, mystery and adventure of a trip back to China. Marco had the same urges.

A Hope and a Pope

Before they ventured too far, they had a problem.
The Great Khan had asked the Polos to deliver 100
Christian priests to China and to gather some holy
oil from Jerusalem. Kublai Khan's mother had been
a Christian, and he was fascinated with Christianity.
He wanted to learn more from experts, like priests.
The Great Khan was interested in many subjects
and all religions. He'd even consider converting to
Christianity, if it appealed to him.

The Polos approached Pope Gregory X, and he
agreed to write a nice, friendly letter to the Khan, but
he would only agree to send two of his friars on the
long, hazardous journey. Bottling up some holy oil in
Jerusalem was a piece of cake compared to finding
priests ready to trek into the unknown.

Soon the Polos and the two reluctant friars were on the road. But it didn't take long for rumours of a war between the Sultans of Babylon and Armenia to circulate and the two priests to refuse to continue on the journey.

Now all the Polos had for Kublai Khan was a letter and holy oil. Was that enough? After all, Kublai Khan was a powerful emperor. Emperors like to get what they want. Would he understand, or would he toss them out of his kingdom — or throw them in jail?

Good Times

The Polos journeyed on with hope and holy water. They travelled through what is now Iran, Iraq and Afghanistan and, on the way, Marco marvelled at wonders he'd never dreamed could exist.

He admired intricately woven carpets, precious stones called turquoises, and the exquisite embroidered silks that he saw in the streets, homes and markets. He sniffed aromatic spices and scented woods. He tasted new foods, including fruits like pomegranate and quince.

He also heard about black oil that gushed from the ground in Baku. "This oil is not good to use with food but is good to burn and cures the mange on camels," he wrote. Marco Polo had stumbled on oil wells that still produce oil today.

Those were the good times.

Tough Times

Then there were the tough times.

The Polos joined a caravan when they neared the land of a nasty robber tribe. They hoped the caravan would protect them from the bandits, but the bandits struck the caravan anyway. The Polos were almost captured and sold into slavery like many of their fellow travellers, but they miraculously escaped.

But that wasn't the end of their hard times.

They crossed a salt desert for eight days, and right after they left that miserable place, they faced an arid plain where there was little water or food.

And then Marco fell sick. Not just a little sick, but very sick for a whole year. As time passed, his dad

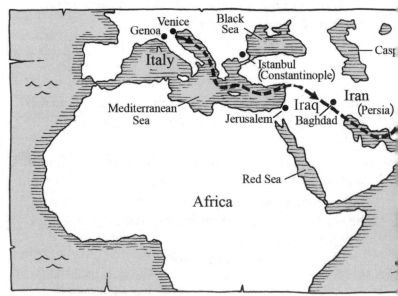

Land journey to Kublai Khan

and uncle were concerned that he wasn't getting any better, and also impatient that they were stuck in the middle of nowhere. Would they ever leave? Would Marco live to meet the Great Khan? Would anyone live to see the Khan?

Then someone had a bright idea. Take Marco up to the mountains where the air is better and there's fresh water. The desperate Polos did just that, and Marco was cured!

But despite the cool air and fresh water, it was time to move on. Before them lay the dreaded Gobi Desert. It would take months to cross the Gobi, and you could go nuts trying.

The desert made strange sounds. There was no

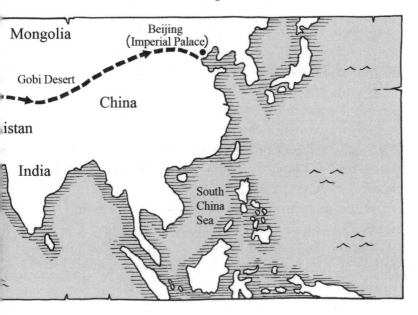

water; there were no animals anywhere — just endless shifting sand. And when you passed the sun-baked bones of travellers who hadn't made it out, shivers crept up your spine. That could be *you*! Like many travellers before them, the Polos were thrilled to see the end of the Gobi.

Hello, Kublai Khan

It was 1275 and the Polos had been on the road for almost four years. They'd been wowed by beautiful places, smelled and savoured spicy new food, faced death by bandits and almost died in the desert. But now they were nearing the Great Khan's summer palace. It was an exciting and terrifying thought.

At last they met Kublai Khan and, to their delight, he understood their problem with the priests. He was a reasonable man and he was glad they'd brought holy oil and a friendly letter from the Pope.

He was also delighted to meet Marco. He thought he was a fine, intelligent young man and was impressed with how quickly he learned new languages. Kublai Khan hired Marco to travel around the enormous Mongol kingdom, check things out and report back what he saw.

What an exciting job! Marco saw *more* awesome sights, like animals "big as elephants, with hair like buffalo, feet like an elephant and a horn in the middle of their forehead." He thought they were unicorns, but Marco had probably seen his first rhinoceros.

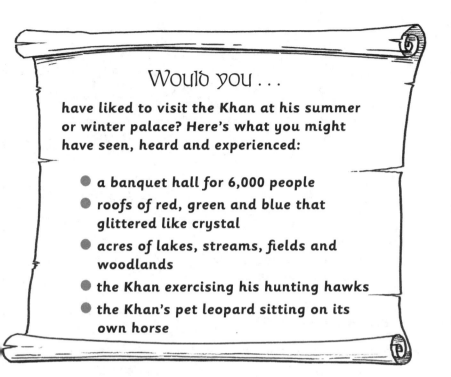

Would you . . .

have liked to visit the Khan at his summer or winter palace? Here's what you might have seen, heard and experienced:

- a banquet hall for 6,000 people
- roofs of red, green and blue that glittered like crystal
- acres of lakes, streams, fields and woodlands
- the Khan exercising his hunting hawks
- the Khan's pet leopard sitting on its own horse

We Want to Go Home!

After 17 years in the Mongol Empire, the Polos worried that Kublai Khan was getting old and that they might not be welcomed by his successor. They decided it was time to go home.

But Kublai Khan didn't want them to leave. It was only after much discussion that they came to an agreement. The Great Khan said that if the Polos would take Princess Kokachin to Persia to meet Arghun, her husband-to-be, they could go back to Venice. Kublai Khan would even give them his golden tablet, which would allow the Polos to travel freely and

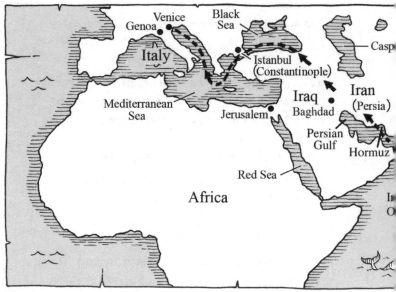

Return sea voyage

find help anywhere. This time they'd travel by sea.

It sounded like a great plan. No more trekking through the Gobi desert. No more bandits. Just a nice sea voyage, which should take them home faster.

It did take them home faster (two years instead of four) but it was a tough trip. They were stranded in Sumatra for months after being caught in torrential rains. They encountered pirates. Disease was rampant aboard the ship and 600 passengers and crew died on that voyage. Luckily the princess, her ladies and the Polos survived.

When they finally arrived at Hormuz on the Persian Gulf, they heard that Arghun had died. Now what? More talk, more worry — but finally it was

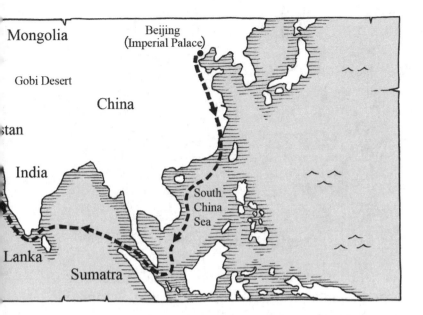

decided that the princess would marry Arghun's son, Prince Ghazan.

After a tearful parting with the princess, the Polos were ready to head to Venice. But before they left, there was one more piece of sad news. Kublai Khan had died. The Polos were relieved they'd left China before the emperor died and thankful they'd known such a great and powerful man.

The Book that Changed Everything

The Polos arrived back in Venice in 1295. Marco had left as a boy of 17. He returned a man of 41.

Three years after he was back, he commanded a galley in a war that Venice waged against its rival city

of Genoa, and Marco was captured and jailed. That's where he met a writer, Rustichello of Pisa. During the long days and nights in jail, Marco told his fellow prisoners about his amazing travels.

Rustichello was enthralled. He insisted that he record the stories and offered to help write them down. So Marco dictated and Rustichello wrote. The book, called *The Description of the World,* sold like hot cakes. It was eventually translated into many languages, including English, in which it was called *The Travels of Marco Polo.*

Marco was released from prison after a year. He married and had three daughters. He lived in Venice till his death in 1324 at the age of 70.

On his deathbed, some people encouraged Marco to admit that he'd fabricated the stories in his book. He refused. He said, "I have only told the half of what I saw."

The Debate Rages On

For the next two centuries, the after-effects of the Black Death, which had ravaged Europe, and restrictions from the Ottoman Empire halted trade between Europe and China. Few Europeans could verify Marco Polo's stories, and many questioned the truth of what Marco claimed he saw and experienced.

The debate about Marco's book and its accuracy has raged on for centuries.

What Do We Think of Marco Polo Now?

So how much of what Marco Polo wrote is true? Why is it that he never mentioned some key aspects of life in China, such as the Great Wall, women's foot binding, calligraphy or tea? Why was his name never mentioned in Chinese records? And to complicate things even more, as the years passed and translations were made of Marco's book, changes were made to the text. No original manuscript even exists today.

So what's true and what's not?

Today more and more historians believe that most of what Marco described actually happened, and much of what he saw was accurate too. Chinese scholars claimed that he recorded aspects of Chinese life that only someone who was there at the time could know.

Here are just a few things that amazed Marco that scholars now agree were true: the Chinese had a postal delivery system, they used paper money and burned their dead.

Marco Polo had an extraordinary journey. He observed much in his 17 years of service to Kublai Khan. Many people thought the East was full of weird creatures and strange people. They were wrong. Marco Polo admired and described a civilization that was very advanced and technologically superior to Europe's.

TRUE OR False?

Many people asserted that Marco Polo's tales were just a pack of lies. Which of these Marco Polo descriptions do you think are true, and which do you think Marco may have heard about and passed on (and are probably not true)?

1. birds that pick up elephants

2. black stones that burn

3. a ruby as big as a fist

4. dog-headed men who eat anything they catch

1. F, 2. T: It was coal. 3. T, 4. F

Report Card

Marco Polo

Daring..*A*

Persistence ....*A*

Getting Along with Others...*A*

Where Are You Going, Columbus?

Christopher Columbus (1451–1506)

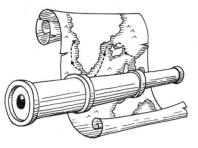

 How do you persuade royalty
to finance your journey into
treacherous, uncharted seas?
1. Flatter them shamelessly.
2. Argue with them endlessly.
3. Dangle the possibility of riches, glory,
   fame or all three.
4. Never take no for an answer.

If you picked any of those four answers, you're
correct. Christopher Columbus tried all four ways to
cajole King Ferdinand and Queen Isabella of Spain
into believing that their investment in his expeditions
would pay off. Did they immediately agree? Were they
pleased with the results of his voyages? Did Columbus
march into retirement rich and famous? What kind of
guy was he, anyway?

Who Was Christopher Columbus?

In 1451, Christopher Columbus was born to a weaver and his wife in Genoa, an Italian seaport. He had red hair and was the oldest of five kids. He lived near the sea and he yearned to sail and have adventures. When he was older, he did.

His first trip out into the Atlantic almost killed him. It was the year 1476, and Columbus was 25 years old and sailing on a trading ship past Portugal when French privateers attacked his ship. Flung into the sea, weak and wounded, Columbus desperately tried to keep afloat while his ship burned and sank.

That might have been the end of him and certainly the end of his dreams of adventure at sea, but Columbus was both lucky and plucky. He grabbed an oar and gradually kicked his way to the Portuguese shore.

He arrived there safely and decided to stay in Portugal. After all, if you were interested in sailing, Portugal was the place to be. It had a long seafaring history, and Portugal's King John was keen on finding a swift route to the Indies, where you could buy spices (needed to improve food in the late 1400s) and acquire jewels and gold.

He also became fascinated by Marco Polo's tales of his adventures in the East and throughout China. Columbus wanted adventure, riches, glory and fame. He was sure he'd achieve it all if he became a successful explorer.

I Know the Way

Unfortunately, in the mid 1400s, the Ottoman Empire made it difficult to travel overland the way the Polos had done in the 1200s. The only way to reach the East now was by ship. That was fine with Columbus. He couldn't wait to sail off again.

But did he take off immediately? No! He did eventually join some expeditions, but he also ran a store, sold maps and talked to sailors and scientists about his ideas and theories. And those theories differed sharply from the opinions most people, including King John, held at the time.

How? Columbus thought that sailing around Africa and then heading east was not going to get anyone to the Spice Islands of Asia quickly. The short cut was to sail west. He was sure about his theory of the power of *las brisas*, the trade winds. He was certain *las brisas* would push his ships faster and farther. Now all Columbus had to do was convince the king that he was right.

But the king and his council weren't buying any of it. For one thing, the King thought Columbus was "a big talker and boastful in setting forth his accomplishments and full of fancy

and imagination." The King's experts felt his plans were too expensive and he was wrong about distances and measurements. Portugal believed in an eastern route to Asia via Africa, not Columbus's western route.

How Do You Speak to a Queen?

Well, if Portugal wasn't interested, Columbus would take his ideas to Spain. After all, the Spanish were keen on catching up to the Portuguese in exploration. They'd love to control new routes and new lands and he, Christopher Columbus, would be the perfect person to make their exploration dreams come true! All he had to do was convince Spain's King Ferdinand and Queen Isabella of his ideas and they'd be delighted to send him off.

What's more, Queen Isabella was an ardent Christian (so ardent that she had people who disagreed with her burned and tortured). She'd like nothing better than to convert the locals to Christianity. Columbus was sure he could do that too.

But how do you get to speak to a king and queen? Network! Cozy up to influential people!

In 1485 Columbus travelled to the southern Spanish port town of Palos de la Frontera, sent his young son Diego to boarding school in the neighbourhood and became acquainted with the local friars. Friar Antonio de Marchena was fascinated by Columbus's ideas, and he introduced Columbus to a powerful nobleman, Hernando de Talavera, who was the queen's spiritual advisor.

What could be better? Queen Isabella's advisor could be a great ally. Now all Columbus had to do was tell the royal couple his ideas and they'd be hooked.

And they *were* intrigued. They liked Columbus's enthusiasm, but they told him his timing was off. They were way too busy fighting the Moors in southern Spain to think about exploration. Columbus would have to wait for them to consider his proposal.

I Don't Want to Wait

Columbus didn't want to wait, but he had no choice. In 1487 he was finally able to present his ideas to a committee of Spanish experts on exploration. But, like the Portuguese, they told him the ocean was too large to cross and refused to endorse his ideas.

Another disappointment! But did that stop Columbus? Not a chance. He talked to more people and, although some laughed at his notions, others were impressed with his ideas and certainly with his persistence and determination.

And then, finally, in 1492 something wonderful happened! The Spaniards won the last battle against the Moors in Granada. Now Columbus could persuade King Ferdinand and Queen Isabella to send him off to explore. This time they had to say yes. He believed that, "if it sticks often enough, a drop of water can wear a hole in a stone." He was going to wear down the king and queen till they gave him the ships he wanted and their royal blessing to sail.

To his delight, Queen Isabella finally said yes. But

although he was happy with this long-awaited news, Columbus felt that, since he'd been kept dangling for so long, he deserved more than a couple of ships. If he was going to deliver the riches of the Indies to Spain, he wanted to be appointed admiral of the Ocean Sea, viceroy and governor of all the lands he'd discover, and be awarded one-tenth of the booty he'd bring back to Spain. And he wanted those rights passed down to his heirs.

The queen was appalled. She was outraged. The nerve of that Columbus! There was no way she was going to give him all that stuff. He could take his ideas and go!

Columbus almost did. He was about to head for France and see if the French would grant him ships and titles, when Queen Isabella had a change of heart. After all, she figured, what could she lose? If he was right, no big deal — she could give Columbus a title and some riches. There would be lots to go around. And if he failed — tough luck for Columbus.

The First Voyage

Columbus was finally ready to sail. He lost no time in outfitting three small ships — the *Pinta*, the *Niña* and the *Santa María*. He recruited 100 sailors, hustled up a bunch of cats to keep the ships' rats down and hired an interpreter to communicate with the locals. He filled his ship with the usual provisions for a sea journey — food, ammunition (in case of unfriendly encounters), firewood, wine, water, some trinkets to trade, a compass and a half-hourglass to mark the time.

And off they sailed. After a brief stop in the Canary Islands to repair a broken cable, they headed into unknown waters. It was September 1492, and the sailors had no idea where they would land, how long it would take or if sea serpents would swallow their ship along the way. They had to trust Columbus.

Enough "*Adelante*"!

They sailed on and on. Days passed. Nights passed. Frustration grew. Okay, there were no sea monsters, but there was endless ocean and endless sky. Just no land.

Columbus knew his sailors were growing weary and angry. They were also growing impatient with his constant order to sail on. "*Adelante!*" (Onward!) he'd proclaim, no matter what happened or how much they complained. *Adelante* worked for a while but, as they sailed on without sighting land, it wasn't enough. What could Columbus do? Lie? Yes! He'd twist the truth and trick the crew to keep the whole expedition from falling apart.

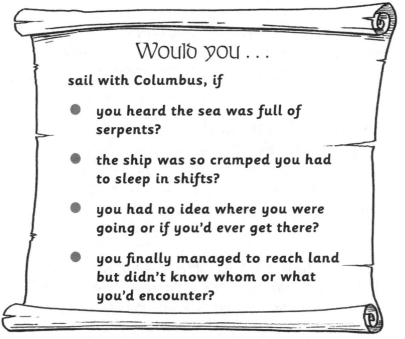

Would you . . .

sail with Columbus, if

- **you heard the sea was full of serpents?**

- **the ship was so cramped you had to sleep in shifts?**

- **you had no idea where you were going or if you'd ever get there?**

- **you finally managed to reach land but didn't know whom or what you'd encounter?**

You Can't Trust Columbus

Columbus told the crew they hadn't really travelled *that* far and that they were almost at their destination. He kept pointing to encouraging signs that land was near, like birds flying near the ship and a live crab tangled in weeds. This deception calmed the crew for a while, but not for long.

Soon Captain Martín Alonso Pinzón of the *Pinta* grew suspicious and accused Columbus of lying. Captain Pinzón and his crew insisted they turn back and head home. Columbus was cornered. Nothing was working now! Not his promise of a reward. Not the branch of berries he said he'd found floating in the sea — another indication that land was close. He was forced to promise the crew that if they didn't reach land in three days, they'd turn back. And to sweeten the deal, he promised to reward the first man to sight land.

Land, but What Land?

On October 11, the sailors spotted some land birds, some driftwood — and then a light in the distance. At 2:00 a.m. on October 12, a sailor on the *Pinta* named Rodrigo de Triana screamed "*Tierra!*" (Land!). Columbus was so relieved and delighted, he fell to his knees.

As for the reward Columbus had promised, poor Rodrigo got almost nothing. Columbus claimed that *he'd* sighted land first from the *Niña*. As you can imagine, Rodrigo was not happy.

Columbus had arrived in what we now call the Bahamas but he was sure was the Indies. He called the place San Salvador and its inhabitants Indians, for

the Indies. Of course, he was surprised that the people and the land weren't quite what he'd expected. The local inhabitants were walking around as naked "as their mother bore them," and there was no sign of gold except in their nose rings.

It was an attractive place, though, full of parrots, multi-coloured fish and tall trees. There were nifty hanging beds (hammocks) and portly mermaids (sea cows). But where was the gold?

Columbus kept searching for it as he sailed around the islands for weeks, claiming all the land for Spain. He claimed what is now Cuba. He claimed what are now Haiti and the Dominican Republic (which he called Hispaniola). Here he was given a chunk of gold by the peaceful Taíno people and he was ecstatic. That proved it! He'd found the Indies. He wasn't sure if it was India, China, Japan or Indonesia — but it was the Indies! Now if only he could find a gold mine, then everything would be perfect. It had to be around here somewhere. He just had to keep looking. But when he sailed off to find more gold, the *Santa Maria* crashed on a reef.

Columbus wasn't happy about the crash, but he wasn't devastated. He figured it was time to head home to Spain anyway, and he still had two ships left. He'd leave 39 men behind in Hispaniola who'd continue the hunt for gold, and he'd report the success of his mission to Queen Isabella and King Ferdinand in person.

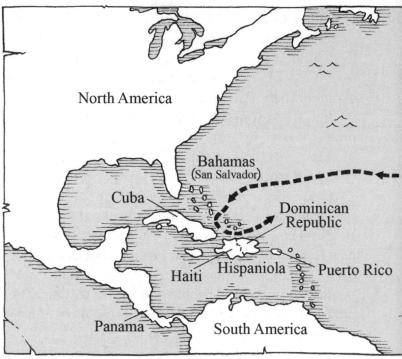

Journey to Hispaniola

Fame and the Second Voyage!

Despite encountering a deadly storm at sea, almost losing the *Pinta* and being detained in Portugal, Columbus returned to Spain triumphant. All the years of cajoling the royal couple had paid off. All the people who'd mocked him now showered him with compliments.

It was a glorious moment and he savoured it. It was lucky he did, because it was downhill for Columbus from then on.

In 1493 he set out on his second voyage, but this

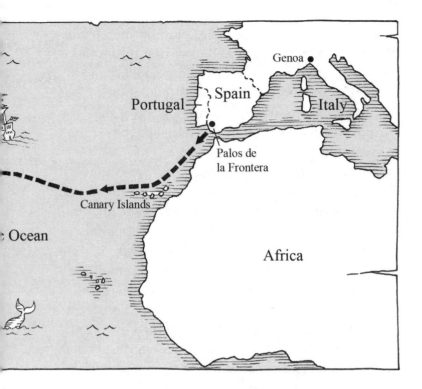

time he was equipped with 17 ships, over 1,200 men, including farmers, soldiers, priests to convert the natives, a bunch of pigs, horses, cattle and sheep, and a pack of dogs.

On the way back to Hispaniola, he had some strange adventures. On one island Columbus and his crew thought the locals were cannibals and hightailed it out of there. On another island, they tasted a scrumptious yellow fruit (pineapple) and were eager to sample the delicious new fruit again.

But the real shock came when they arrived in

Hispaniola. All 39 of the men Columbus had left at the fort had been killed. And after that things just got worse. The settlers Columbus had brought along to work the land refused to do anything but look for gold, and then many of them got sick. On top of that, the Taínos weren't the least bit interested in converting to Christianity.

What should Columbus do? There was little gold around and no gold mines. What if he hadn't found the Indies after all? What would he tell the king and queen? The king had never been a big supporter of Columbus's ambitions. It was the queen who'd almost always backed him up. He had to bring something back to her.

So Columbus rounded up 500 Taínos and decided to sell them as slaves in Spain. And then he forced more of them to pan for gold in the riverbeds. When they produced little, he punished them. Columbus was unhappy, desperate and turning mean.

Finally Columbus returned to Spain, but this time his reception was cool and skeptical. Why hadn't he found gold? Had he really discovered the fast way east or was he a fraud?

The Shame of the Third Voyage
On May 30, 1498, Columbus set sail again. Again the trip was fraught with hardships, and this time the heat was so intense on the voyage that the crew felt as though they'd all burn to a crisp.

And for the next two years as governor of

Hispaniola, Columbus dealt with revolt, disease, corruption and misery. He didn't make matters any better with his attitude as a leader. The locals hated the way he governed. There were endless complaints, and the King and Queen of Spain sent an emissary to check out what was going on.

The emissary arrived to find seven Spaniards dangling from the gallows. They'd revolted, and this was their punishment. The emissary was so shocked that he didn't ask what happened. He simply had Columbus bound in chains and hauled him back to Spain.

The chains were removed before Columbus saw the queen, but by now he was exhausted and sick with arthritis. Yet, as always, he was determined. He begged to return one more time to the islands his ships

had reached. The king and queen granted Columbus his wish but told him not to go near Hispaniola. He was not welcome there ever again.

The Fourth and Last Voyage

Did he listen? Not Columbus! Despite the royal orders, he tried to land in Hispaniola and was refused. So he sailed off to see what else he could find in the neighbourhood. He travelled as far as modern-day Panama. Little did he know that he was near the Pacific, a vast ocean that separated him from the *real* Japan and China. All he knew was that he had failed to find the riches and the glory that he so desperately wanted. And he was sick again, this time with malaria.

Columbus had finally had enough. He headed back to Spain. He wanted to explain to Queen Isabella how hard he'd tried and that he really had succeeded in his quest. But the Queen died before he could see her.

Until the day that Columbus himself died in 1506, he still believed he'd discovered a route to the Indies. True, the place wasn't exactly what he'd hoped for and, true, there were some unexpected wrinkles in his plans, but he knew he'd landed somewhere special. And if it wasn't the Indies, what was it?

What Do We Think of Columbus Today?

Christopher Columbus was not the first European to land in North America. The Vikings preceded him.

But even though he never reached the Spice Islands, he was a skilled seaman who successfully sailed to North America four times. His voyages inspired other explorers to sail to the New World. But his actions widened the slave trade and brought disease and misery to the native population.

. The contact between Europe and the Americas would never be the same after Columbus.

Report Card

Christopher Columbus

Daring..A

Persistence..A

Getting Along with Others..D+

GIMME! GIMME! GOLD AND GLORY

HERNÁN CORTÉS (1485–1547)

POP

QUIZ To conquer tl
Mexico you should . . .
1. learn the Mexican hat dance.
2. drink gallons of spicy Aztec chocolate.
3. wear clunky armour.
4. be ruthless and sneaky.

If you picked answers 2, 3 or 4, you're right.
Drinking spicy Aztec chocolate would endear you to
Emperor Montezuma II, who guzzled it down. And
Hernán Cortés, one of the most brilliant, brutal and
bold conquistadors ever, vanquished the Aztecs despite
wearing clunky armour.

Conquistador means "one who conquers" in
Spanish, and that's just what Cortés set out to do.
Nothing was going to stop him. Not respect for a
great civilization like the Aztecs — people who'd built
amazing cities and a culture rich with art and music.

Not Aztec emperors who treated him like a god. Not even heavy armour on a hot day. Cortés wanted riches, fame and power. He claimed, "We Spaniards suffer from a disease that only gold can cure."

How did Cortés conquer a huge empire with only a bunch of horses, a couple of hundred men and some guns?

Who was Hernán Cortés?

Cortés was born in Medellín in the Extremadura province of Spain in 1485. He was seven years old when Christopher Columbus sailed off to the new world. Columbus's famous journey would trigger Cortés's ambitions and influence his life and career.

Cortés came from a family of hidalgos, or minor nobility, but his family didn't have much money. He was sickly as a child and the only son in the family. When he was 14, the family shipped him off to Salamanca University to become a lawyer.

The only trouble was he didn't want to become a lawyer. He didn't want to sit around reading books all day, arguing cases or studying. Cortés was restless. The tales of explorers like Columbus mesmerized him, and he yearned to sail off to find riches, spices and new lands.

Dropout

After two years at university, he dropped out. His parents were not pleased. They were sure that his reckless nature and haughty attitude were going to land him in trouble. They were right.

It wasn't that Cortés was lazy. He knew he had to get a job, and he knew that there weren't many options for a young man from a family without much money. He could either join the military or head to the New World to seek his fortune there. Cortés decided to check out the opportunities in the New World.

He hoped to head for the island of Hispaniola, where Columbus had landed 12 years earlier. But Cortés never made it to Hispaniola. He missed his boat! He'd been out gallivanting the night before and fell off a wall while visiting a lady friend. He was not just late but wounded.

It took a year for him to recover and reorganize. Then he tried to ship out again. This time he succeeded. After a miserable voyage across the sea, Cortés reached Hispaniola and began to work as a clerk.

Like a lot of Spanish newcomers to the New World in those days, he was given free land. He liked owning land, but not farming it. "I came to get gold," he said, "not to till the soil like a peasant." He forced the local Taínos to work the land while he trained as a soldier and fought duels over ladies. (Cortés always liked the ladies!) In one duel, he was wounded under his chin and had to grow a beard to hide his slashed face.

TRUE OR False?

The Spanish province of Extremadura shaped the lives of so many daring conquistadores like Hernán Cortés, Francisco Pizarro and Vasco Núñez de Balboa because of

1. something in the water.

2. something in the food.

3. poverty in the province.

4. the way each explorer's exploits influenced others.

Answers: 1. F, 2. F, 3. T, 4. T

Hothead in Trouble!

In 1511 Cortés took part in a battle to conquer Cuba and was rewarded with more land by Spanish commander Diego Velázquez, who'd sailed with Columbus on his second voyage. Cortés was also appointed mayor of Santiago, Cuba. Pretty good for a pale, bowlegged, black-bearded 26-year-old. But despite his success, his ambition and hotheadedness continued to land him in trouble.

He had a dispute with Velázquez and was tossed in jail. But soon the two men reconciled, and Cortés married Catalina, Velázquez's sister-in-law.

Did Cortés settle down now? Was he satisfied with his prestigious job, a thriving estate and a pretty new wife? Not Cortés.

What he really wanted to do was fight and conquer. In 1519 he convinced Velázquez to let him lead an expedition to what we now call Mexico, which was ruled by the Aztec emperor Montezuma II. Word of the riches and splendour of the Aztec empire had filtered out and fired up the imagination of gold-hungry Spaniards like Cortés and Velázquez.

Velázquez insisted that Cortés claim any land only for Spain — not for himself. He directed him to search for shipwrecked sailors from a previous expedition along the way, and he warned Cortés that he must treat the native population well.

Ha Ha! Can't Catch Me!

Cortés agreed to Velázquez's conditions but, despite his agreement, he had no intention of following through. He soon made elaborate travel preparations, including ordering a fancy embroidered banner declaring, "We will conquer." He solicited soldiers by promising them wealth and took along so many supplies he had to mortgage his property.

Velázquez got suspicious. Why did Cortés need to take so much stuff on this expedition? Could he want to do more than claim the land for Spain? Perhaps he wanted to conquer the land for himself!

Velázquez couldn't let that wily Cortés succeed
with his underhanded scheme! No way! He'd stop him
before he sailed off.

But it was too late. Before Velázquez could prevent
him from leaving, Cortés and his men shipped out.
They were bound for the Aztec empire and its gold and
glory, and Cortés had no plans to share the wealth
with Velázquez.

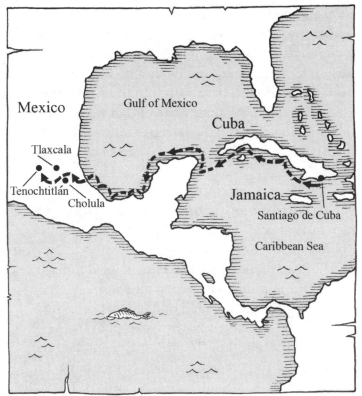

Journey to the Aztec capital

Conquistador on the Loose!

Cortés assembled 11 ships, about 16 horses, some cannons and over 650 men armed with crossbows and field guns. He knew that before he could strike a powerful empire like the Aztecs, he needed help from people who spoke the local language.

After brutally conquering the local Tabascan tribe, Cortés used Malinche, a local woman who spoke both the Mayan and Aztec languages, to translate for him.

Meanwhile, the Aztecs heard about Cortés and sent a representative named Teudile to find out what he was up to. Cortés told Teudile that he was on a mission from the King of Spain to speak to the Aztec emperor, Montezuma II. Of course, none of that was true. Cortés was not planning to talk. He was planning to conquer the Aztecs, but he hoped he could do so by outwitting them.

Teudile said the emperor could not come to talk but, as a welcoming gesture, he gave Cortés and his men gifts of gold. The Aztecs hoped the Spaniards would take the loot and leave. Teudile also lit incense and, to the Spaniards' astonishment, bled himself and offered the Spaniards his blood on straws.

Despite the gifts of gold and blood, Cortés had no intention of going anywhere except to the Aztec capital of Tenochtitlán. To prove his point, he fired his cannons and ordered his men to race down the beach on horses, brandishing their swords. The Aztecs, who'd never seen horses before and had never heard

cannons, were so terrified that they fell trembling to the ground.

Now the Aztecs were really worried. Not only did these strangers have powerful weapons and horrific animals, but their leader Cortés might be the god Quetzalcoatl, who was supposed to return to Aztec land. He certainly *looked* like their god. According to their legends, Quetzalcoatl was bearded, with pale skin, and came from across the water. And if he returned, legend said, it might mean the end of the Aztecs.

What should they do? What *could* they do? How could they get rid of these guys?

The Aztecs decided to shower the Spaniards with more gold. But it didn't help. The Spaniards still wouldn't leave.

Too Many Aztecs, Cortés!

Meanwhile, some of Cortés's men were worried too. There were a lot more Aztecs than Spaniards. They didn't want to be killed by the Aztecs. Maybe they should head back. But Cortés refused to turn back. How could he? If he returned to Cuba, he'd be in trouble with Velázquez for violating his orders. He might be arrested, maybe hanged.

Cortés decided instead that they should set up a colony right where they were, and he'd resign from Velázquez's expedition. He'd be in charge of their new settlement and, from then on, his only allegiance would be to the King of Spain, not Velázquez. He also arranged to send all the loot they'd received from the Aztecs to the king, to prove his allegiance.

Then, to make absolutely sure none of his men tried to sail back to Cuba, Cortés secretly sank all the ships. With no ships, they had no choice but to "conquer or die."

Imagine how stunned Cortés's men were at that news! They were marooned in a strange land. But what could they do? Nothing but follow their clever, ruthless conquistador.

And to make sure he'd succeed, Cortés had local allies: he fought, vanquished and then befriended a local tribe called the Tlaxcalans, who hated the Aztecs. (The Aztecs not only taxed the Tlaxcalans heavily but demanded human sacrifices.)

Together with the Tlaxcalans, the Spaniards then fought and massacred the Cholulans, another local tribe. The Spaniards' reputation as fierce and ruthless warriors was spreading through the Aztec empire.

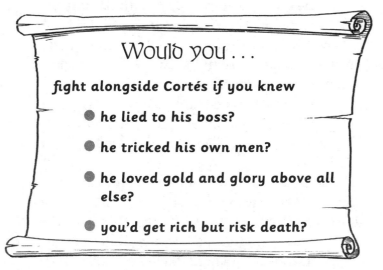

Woulδ you ...

fight alongside Cortés if you knew

● **he lied to his boss?**

● **he tricked his own men?**

● **he loved gold and glory above all else?**

● **you'd get rich but risk death?**

Watch Out! The Conquistador Is Coming!

Cortés began marching toward Tenochtitlán, the Aztec capital. Along the way, he killed more tribes and made new allies.

And then he saw the Aztec capital! It was magnificent! It was built on an island surrounded by a lake. There were huge markets selling spices and strange foods. There were canals transporting goods. The gardens, the orchards, the ponds were stunning. It was also cleaner than any Spanish city.

And there was Emperor Montezuma II borne on the shoulders of his lords. He had pierced ears, a pierced lower lip and a pierced nose. He wore a cape, feathers and jewel-studded shoes. Cortés and the emperor greeted each other cautiously.

Montezuma had decided to try to placate the tough Cortés. He gave the Spaniards beautiful apartments to stay in and more jewels and gold.

The two leaders spoke through their interpreters. They tried to be respectful to each other, but there was always lingering mistrust.

As the weeks passed and the Spaniards craved more gold and began interfering with the Aztecs' religion, tensions grew. Montezuma was caught in the middle.

Cortés decided to do something dramatic to show the Aztecs who was their real boss. He insisted that Montezuma stay at the palace provided for the Spaniards. In effect, he took Montezuma hostage.

Montezuma acquiesced. Maybe he had no real choice any more. Maybe he knew that if he didn't, the Spaniards might kill him.

Montezuma's actions only made things worse. The Aztecs lost respect for their leader.

Then one day soon after, Cortés and his men went too far. They struck down the Aztec idols with iron bars. They melted down Aztec gold used to honour their gods. They started to put up Christian crosses. The Aztecs were livid.

While all this was going on in Tenochtitlán, back in Cuba Governor Velázquez heard about Cortés's exploits. He was furious. He was determined to stop the upstart conquistador from seizing new land and acquiring more Aztec gold. Velázquez sent soldiers to capture Cortés.

Enemies Everywhere

Soon it would be Spaniard against Spaniard in the middle of Aztec territory. What could Cortés do? He had enemies everywhere.

He came up with a cunning plan. He'd surprise Velázquez's men and attack them at night. But first he had to leave someone in charge in Tenochtitlán. He gave the job to a hotheaded Spaniard named Pedro de Alvarado.

The surprise attack on Velázquez's troops worked! Cortés beat Velázquez's men, and when Velázquez's surviving soldiers eyed all the gold that Cortés's men had acquired, many changed sides and joined Cortés's forces.

Things were looking up! Cortés had a bigger army now. All he had to do was go back to Tenochtitlán and he'd be in charge of the Aztec capital, without waving a sword or firing a cannon.

But things went awry. While Cortés was fighting Velázquez's men, his deputy in Tenochtitlán, Alvarado, panicked. He thought the Aztecs were about to assault him, and he ordered an attack on them during an important Aztec religious ceremony. Soon a full-blown battle took place.

Cortés returned to find the bridges destroyed and the Spaniards unable to obtain food or water. And when the Spaniards forced Montezuma to speak to his people, he was bombarded with rocks and arrows by the furious Aztecs. Soon after, Montezuma died.

Destroy and Conquer

The battle raged on for months under Montezuma's brother Cuitláhuac. The Spaniards almost starved. They almost gave up. And when many tried to flee clutching their gold, they were killed or drowned. The situation was desperate, and Cortés was forced to regroup outside the city.

For a while, all was calm within Tenochtitlán. Although Emperor Cuitláhuac soon died of smallpox, the Aztecs chose a young new emperor called Cuauhtémoc and resumed their old way of life. They hoped those vicious Spaniards had finally had enough and had left for good.

But everything changed again as smallpox, the terrible disease that killed Emperor Cuitláhuac, spread rapidly in the Aztec capital. Many Aztecs died. The Spaniards had unintentionally brought a horrible disease to the Aztec people.

Meanwhile outside the Aztec capital, Cortés was planning his next move. He figured the key to success was to use the lake surrounding Tenochtitlán to conquer the city. So he built ships, and the Spaniards sailed closer and closer to the capital. Then they struck.

They rammed the Aztecs' canoes. They deployed their cannons and lances. They fought street by street. The Aztecs fought bravely, but it was no use. What made it worse was that there were fewer Aztecs to fight since so many had died of smallpox. And they didn't have guns or horses like the Spaniards.

Cortés destroyed the magnificent Aztec city of Tenochtitlán. Over 200,000 Aztecs perished. On August 13, 1521, the great Aztec empire fell.

What Now, Cortés?

In 1522, to Cortés's delight, he was appointed governor, captain general and chief justice of what was now called New Spain by King Charles V. He'd achieved it all! He was on top of the world.

He rebuilt Tenochtitlán and renamed it Mexico City. But not all his plans worked out so well. He sent expeditions to seek out new territory, but the only valuable land discovered was what is now Baja California. When he sent an expedition to Honduras, the leader of that expedition turned against him.

Cortés was also getting older. All these new battles were tiring him out. How long could a conquistador fight?

Soon old enemies resurfaced. People accused Cortés of murder. He returned to Spain to clear his name and, at first, it worked. The king believed him! He even rewarded him with new land in West Mexico and a fancy new title. But the king refused to allow him to govern New Spain again.

Cortés even tried to live a quiet life, but the old restlessness crept in. Even though he was older and weaker, he was still a conquistador in his heart, and conquistadors live to fight and explore. When the new governor of New Spain refused to let Cortés explore further into South America, Cortés returned to Spain to plead his case again with the king.

But this time the king didn't care. He was too busy with other troubles in Spain to bother with a tired, aging explorer.

Cortés was crushed. He prepared to return to New Spain for the last time, but he never made it back. He died in Spain on December 2, 1547.

What Do We Think of Cortés Today?

Historians marvel at Cortés's cunning, bravado and skill. In a short time, with few men, he was able to conquer a huge empire. But, in so doing, he destroyed an amazing civilization and a beautiful city with lush gardens, clean water and good plumbing. He also opened the gates to the further subjugation of the indigenous people.

No wonder Cortés's name is reviled in Mexico. In 1821 Mexicans tried to dig up his bones and destroy them. And today there isn't a single statue of Cortés in all of Mexico.

Report Card

Hernán Cortés

Daring..A
Persistence..A
Getting Along with Others.................................F

Cheer Up!
It Could Be Worse

Samuel de Champlain (*circa* 1570–1635)

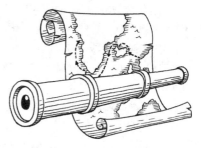

POP QUIZ How do you survive in the 1600s in a new land with little food and long, icy winters?

1. Stay under your quilt for six months.
2. Throw parties to distract yourself.
3. Eat fruits and vegetables so you don't develop scurvy, which would make your teeth rot.
4. Go somewhere else fast.

If you picked answers 2, 3 or 4, you're right. When explorer Samuel de Champlain started a colony in what is now Canada, he and his men had to figure out all that and more. No Europeans in those days knew how to cure scurvy. (The Native North Americans did!) Many sailors and colonists became sick and died from that awful disease.

Good thing Champlain knew how to throw a good party. His colonist get-togethers cheered everyone up.

For a while they forgot they were cold, hungry and miserable.

Of course Champlain didn't have parties all the time. He was too busy exploring, map-making and travelling back and forth between France and the New World.

Over the years, Champlain sailed across the Atlantic Ocean over 21 times — an amazing feat at a time when sea travel was uncomfortable, unpleasant and dangerous.

How did he do it? And how did he stay good-humoured and trustworthy, when so many other explorers were ruthless or unreliable?

Who was Samuel de Champlain?

We know a lot about Champlain's expeditions and colonies through his writings. We know little about his private life because he hardly mentioned it.

What we do know is that Samuel Champlain was born around 1570 in a small coastal town in France called Brouage. He came from a family of sea captains. The sea was in Champlain's blood — and so was wanderlust.

He was fascinated by the stories of Columbus, Cortés and Champlain's fellow Frenchman, Jacques Cartier. Champlain figured that if you wanted to make it BIG in France, especially if you didn't inherit wealth or power, you'd better be bold and adventurous.

But in the late 1500s, France wasn't interested in explorers. The country was too busy fighting religious wars between Protestants and Catholics. Champlain decided that if he couldn't explore, he'd become a soldier and fight with King Henry IV against the Catholic League.

He learned a lot as a soldier. He learned how to take care of himself in freezing temperatures, how to survive on little food, how to persevere through tough times and how to ambush an enemy. He also learned how important it was to work as a team.

He distinguished himself as a soldier and rose up in the ranks of command. Even the King of France noticed how good he was at his job.

I Love Mexico

When France's war was finally over, Champlain was in his early thirties. What next? Follow his dream and explore, of course!

But how should he start? Where should he go? France was still not interested in exploration. Spain, on the other hand, had encouraged explorers for over a hundred years. Columbus and Cortés had explored for Spain. And while they did, Columbus had stumbled onto the New World, and Cortés had conquered the Aztecs' civilization and claimed their land, Mexico, for Spain.

So Champlain headed to Spain to learn everything he could about exploring. Then he hopped on a ship bound for Mexico to check the New World out for himself.

Champlain loved Mexico. He marvelled at the

beautiful trees, the colourful birds, the big turtles, the hungry crocodiles and the slithering rattlesnakes. He relished the variety of fruit and vegetables. He admired Mexico City, with its palaces and temples.

But he was also appalled at the cruel way the indigenous people were treated by the Spanish. The native people were often forced to work as slaves and beaten if they didn't attend church. In Champlain's diary, he recorded and drew pictures of everything he saw and experienced.

Thanks for the "de"!

After more than two years away, Champlain returned to France. He showed his drawings and described his travels in Mexico to King Henry IV. The King was impressed, thanked him for his previous service as a soldier — and gave him a "de" to add to his name. From then on, he would be known as Samuel *de* Champlain, which meant he was nobility in France.

Now that the fighting was over, the king was interested in exploration, only not to Mexico, but to New France. New France was full of possibilities. Beaver felt hats were all the rage in Europe, and Canadian beavers made terrific hats. And, of course, there

was always a chance that one could reach the East Indies and China by way of New France. If Champlain could pull that off, the king would be very happy.

Once a Beaver — Now a Hat

In 1603 Champlain joined a fur merchant named François Gravé and sailed to New France. Champlain liked New France immediately.

He loved the mighty rivers, the thick forests and the variety of animals (especially the furry ones). He understood what the king meant about beavers. They were all over the place. As before, Champlain kept notes and drew pictures of what he saw and what he experienced.

Champlain returned to France and reported back to King Henry again. The king was pleased: Now how about building a colony in Canada? It wasn't going to be easy of course. Previous colonies had failed. But Champlain was a smart fellow. The king was sure he could do better.

Champlain liked the idea, and he too was sure he could make a colony succeed. He would study the past attempts and find out what had gone wrong.

When he investigated, he discovered that the previous colonies had flopped for six reasons. The leaders of the colony hadn't: (1) taken enough useful stuff, (2) explored the land carefully before building, (3) maintained law and order, (4) gotten to know the locals and learned from them, (5) picked a good site for their colony and (6) kept the support of the nobles and rulers in France. Samuel de Champlain was determined to take all these lessons to heart and do better.

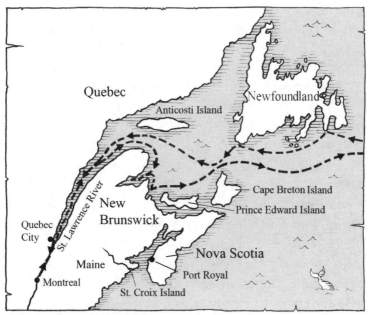

First voyage to New France

So What Do You Think of Life in Acadia Now, Champlain?

In 1604, under the sponsorship of a nobleman named Pierre Du Gua de Monts, Champlain returned to New France to help start the colony of Acadia on Saint Croix Island, near a river between what is now New Brunswick, Canada, and Maine, U.S.A. One hundred and twenty men, including carpenters and blacksmiths, joined him. They began to build houses, storehouses and gardens. Everything started out well. The island looked like a perfect spot for a colony.

Seventy-nine men stayed for the winter, and that's when the trouble began. No one expected winter to be so fierce and so long. Giant slabs of ice isolated the colony. The river froze. Food froze. Cider and wine froze. The men's toes froze. By the end of the winter, only 11 of the 79 men were in decent health. Many had died of starvation and disease. Who knew it would turn out like this?

Despite that terrible experience, Champlain and his remaining men were convinced they could find a better place for a colony. They found one across the bay at Port Royal, in what is now Nova Scotia. Here Champlain had a log stockade built that he called the Habitation, and soon made friends with the local Mi'kmaq. He knew they were experts on how to live there. Having friends like the Mi'kmaq could help the colonists survive through tough times in an unfamiliar new land.

And there was one more thing that would help them through tough times — a few laughs, good food and some fun. So Champlain started The Order of Good Cheer. Everyone took turns cooking new foods like beaver tails, moose pie, bears and otters. They swore that the food and the company were better than anything anywhere — even in Paris!

Over the next few years, Champlain helped keep the Acadia colony going at Port Royal. He also explored and mapped the Atlantic coastline. Then suddenly in 1607 his patron, Pierre de Monts ordered the colonists to close down and head back to France. De Monts thought the location of the colony was a disaster, especially since they weren't trading enough fur. And fur was what it was all about. Fur was what made people rich.

Quebec! Quebec!
What a Wonderful Place!

After a heart-to-heart talk back in France with King Henry and Pierre de Monts, Champlain was allowed to return to the New World to start a new colony. He chose the site of Quebec, (which comes from

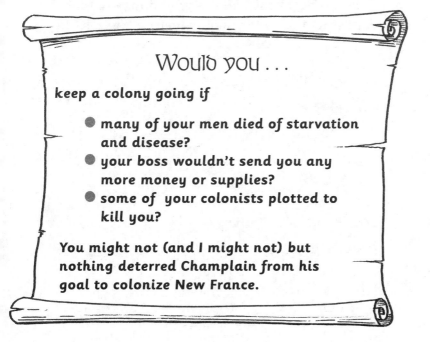

Would you . . .

keep a colony going if

- many of your men died of starvation and disease?
- your boss wouldn't send you any more money or supplies?
- some of your colonists plotted to kill you?

You might not (and I might not) but nothing deterred Champlain from his goal to colonize New France.

the Algonquin word meaning narrow passage or strait) as a place he thought would be perfect for a colony. It overlooked the St. Lawrence River, and the height would be good for defence in case of attack. Champlain set to work building his second Habitation.

But soon there were problems at Habitation 2. Some disgruntled colonists who felt they were overworked hatched a plot to kill Champlain. Lucky for Champlain, he discovered the plot in time, and the plotters were sentenced to death.

And if that wasn't enough, winter brought freezing weather, food supplies ran short and dysentery and scurvy set in. Only 8 of the 27 men at Quebec survived till the spring. Despite all the effort and pain the colonists had put into building their Habitation, they

were hungry, sick and had traded hardly any furs. It was another disappointment and disaster.

But Champlain wasn't giving up. He figured the reason they hadn't traded furs was because the Native peoples were too busy fighting with each other. The Huron and Algonquin tribes were battling the Iroquois to the south. Once all that fighting stopped, surely the tribes would trade with the French colonists. And if he helped the northerly tribes defeat the Iroquois, fur trading would resume faster.

But what if the Iroquois won? Only a few of Champlain's men were willing to get in the middle of that messy battle. Champlain felt he had no choice. He'd fight!

Ready! Aim! Fire!

In July 1609, Champlain joined the Huron to fight the Iroquois. He wore armour and a helmet and carried his harquebus, a heavy gun. The Iroquois were startled when they saw Champlain in his soldier getup. They'd never seen anything quite like it. He must have looked like an alien to them.

As they lifted their bows to shoot him, Champlain fired his gun. He instantly killed two Iroquois chiefs. The noise and the results were so deafening and horrifying that the Iroquois fled in terror. From that moment on, the Iroquois hated the French.

Soon there were more battles with the fierce and determined Iroquois. Champlain and the northern tribes battled them again the next year. This time

Champlain was shot in the neck. But an arrow in the neck was not going to stop this Frenchman!

Champlain recovered from his injury but soon had to face terrible news. The fur trade was still not thriving, and King Henry of France had been assassinated. Could things get any worse?

Shooting the Rapids

Despite the setbacks, Champlain was as determined, brave and optimistic as ever. His Huron allies were especially impressed when he agreed to shoot the Lachine Rapids with them — even though Champlain, like a lot of sailors in those days, didn't know how to swim. Somehow he managed to stay afloat in those wild and treacherous waters.

In the years that followed, Champlain continued to cross the Atlantic, sailing back and forth between New France and France. He also wrote books, kept journals and drew more maps.

He even got married, although that didn't turn

out too well. His wife was young and, after four years in Quebec, she was desperate to go back to France. It was too lonely and isolated in New France for a young woman.

Life in the Wild Is — Wild

Champlain's problems never seemed to end. The fur trade never took off the way everyone had hoped. Another battle against the Iroquois failed in 1615, and this time Champlain was wounded in the leg and had to be carried off the battlefield.

After that battle, he spent a year with the Huron. While he hung around with them, he learned more about hunting and surviving in the wilderness. He also enjoyed the beauty of the trees and wildflowers. He liked the Huron game of lacrosse.

He respected much about the Huron values, culture and skill. He admired their keen sense of justice and how they were always "faithful to their oaths."

But not everything about the Huron way of life impressed him. They were merciless to their prisoners and often tortured them. They also loved to gamble, sometimes even gambling their wives away.

A Roller Coaster Ride

As the years rolled on, Champlain continued championing the colonies of New France in Quebec to the new king, Louis XIII, and the French nobles. Sometimes they were enthusiastic about his latest plans. Sometimes they dismissed his ideas and refused to help.

Some years the colonists starved in Quebec, while in other years they thrived. Colonizing the New World was a roller coaster ride, but Samuel de Champlain never jumped off.

Even when the English almost conquered Quebec in 1628, and the French colonists were hauled back to England, Champlain remained steadfast. To his joy, at the very last minute, an agreement was reached between the French and the English, and Quebec remained French.

Samuel de Champlain never gave up on his beloved Quebec. He returned for the last time in 1633. He knew he wanted to live for the rest of his life in the place that he'd mapped and explored and loved — and he did. He died in Quebec on December 25th, 1635.

What Do We Think of Champlain Today?

Champlain was a fearless captain, explorer and commander. He crossed the Atlantic so many times, but only once did a ship he was sailing on sink in a storm. Luckily everyone on board survived because of Champlain's quick actions and courage.

Champlain's colony of New France established a European presence in Canada. Despite all the hardships and disappointments, he never gave up on his goals. His tireless efforts, his ability to learn and adapt to new conditions, his detailed maps, skilful drawings and vivid descriptions of what are now five U.S. states and six Canadian provinces were invaluable to future colonists and explorers.

Report Card

Samuel
de Champlain

Daring..A
Persistence...A
Getting Along With Others..A

Misery and Mutiny

Henry Hudson (*circa* 1570–1611)

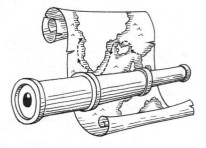

QUIZ How do you provoke a mutiny?

1. Head your ship into nowhere. (Icy, barren nowheres are particularly good at making your crew miserable.)
2. Boss your crew around.
3. Take along a man who hates you already.

If you picked answers 1, 2 or 3 you're right. Henry Hudson had to deal with mutinies throughout his career. So why did he keep sailing? Why did he take his arch enemy on almost all of his journeys? Why did he keep on exploring — leading one disastrous expedition after another? Was he intrepid, obsessed, desperate, persistent, curious, stubborn or short-sighted?

Who Was Henry Hudson?

His story begins in England, probably not far from London. Why probably? Because there's very little known about his early years. Historians figure that he was born around 1570. It's believed that his family were merchants who were part of the Muscovy Company who traded with Russia.

There's a good chance that he sailed with the Muscovy Company before he captained his own ships in 1607. That's when he began to search for the northern passage to the riches and spices of Asia. And that's when he started to write it all down in his journal.

By the time Hudson started to record his adventures, he was 37, married to a woman named Katherine and the father of three boys. He lived near the Tower of London in a small house. Unfortunately, there were no pictures of Hudson made during his lifetime, but one of his contemporaries said he was fair-haired and thin.

Go North, Explorer!

Why did the English want explorers like Hudson to head north to find a route to the East, instead of south? The north was the best (and maybe only) way, because the Spanish and Portuguese had the southern sea route locked up. There were also more pirates looting ships going south.

The English map-makers and explorers were convinced a northern route would work. Sure, you had to sail through icy waters, frigid temperatures and a barren wasteland. Sure, you didn't know how far the ice extended, but the summer sun shone for 24 hours in the Far North. A lot of that thick ice would certainly melt, and then all you needed to do was push your way through it, contend with a bit of fog and you'd be in the sunny East! Then you and your country would reap the riches of the spice lands.

Surprise! Surprise!

Of course, Henry Hudson, his Muscovy employers and the experts of the time didn't know that their theory was full of holes, not to mention ice. They would send Hudson off on a barque (a small wooden ship with three masts) to check out their theory and the northern route. The ship was named *Hopewell*, and that made sense for a ship that was sailing more on a hopeful theory than on reality.

Would you . . .

sail on the *Hopewell?* It had

- **cramped sleeping quarters,**
- **food that spoiled quickly and then crawled with maggots,**
- **water stored in casks that developed a layer of scum on top,**
- **no warmth anywhere, any time.**

Even Henry Hudson had reservations about the expedition. He wrote, "I take leave of England in a few months to test the theory that a route to Cathay [another name for China] can be found across the half-frozen seas that cover the roof of the world. The hopes of my employers are higher than mine that this venture will succeed. I fear the ice may prove too thick."

But despite his worry, he went. He had to. He was drawn to exploration like a bee to a flower. "I would that my name be carved on the tablets of the sea," he wrote.

Hudson and his crew left London on May 1, 1607, and sailed to northwest Greenland. Hudson wanted to map its unexplored parts, but the fog was so thick they couldn't see anything, let alone map it. They had to sail on blindly. Worse still, the sails and riggings became so wet that they froze. The crew sliced their hands trying to move them.

Finally the *Hopewell* managed to sail to a spot called Spitsbergen, which is less than 930 kilometers (500 miles) from the North Pole. That's where they saw an amazing sight. The sea was filled with whales. Some whales even bumped up against the ship!

When the *Hopewell* sailed on, it was totally blocked by ice. There was no way through it, and Hudson finally decided it was time to turn around and head back. He was sure this was not the route to the East. He was confident that there were other routes that were better.

His employers were disappointed that he hadn't found the way to the spice lands, but they were thrilled

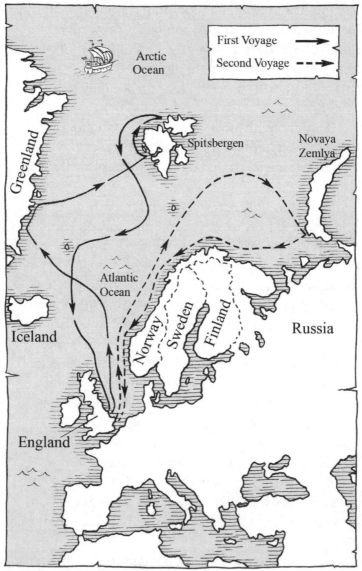

First Voyage →
Second Voyage ⇢

Arctic
Ocean

Greenland

Spitsbergen

Novaya
Zemlya

Atlantic
Ocean

Iceland

Norway

Sweden

Finland

Russia

England

Voyages of the *Hopewell*

to hear about all those whales. Whale hunting was big business in the 1600s. Whales were used for fuel, food and candles, and for clothing like corsets and hoop skirts. Soon whalers converged on Spitsbergen and decimated the whale population.

Whining and Arguing

In 1608, Hudson was ready to try for Asia again. He'd again captain the *Hopewell* for the Muscovy Company, but this time he insisted they reinforce the ship with more planks. The company balked. It was expensive to use more wood, they insisted, but Hudson stood his ground. After all, he and his crew were the ones risking their lives in the ice and sea, he told them. He needed a better, safer ship.

Hudson got his planks. Now he needed a crew. Among the men he hired was Robert Juet, who would serve as first mate — an important job, second only to the captain. Juet was an experienced sailor, ten years older than Hudson, more educated than most sailors and a good navigator. He was also jealous, cynical and quarrelsome.

Hudson knew Juet was a pain from day one. He wrote that Juet was "filled with mean tempers." When Hudson asked him to cut and sew a new sail, he objected that it was beneath him to do that kind of work. He whined and complained about everything, but Hudson didn't fire him. Hudson would later regret that decision.

Mermaids and Lies

Along with Juet and a small crew, Hudson took the *Hopewell* to the northeast. This time he hoped to connect with the Pacific by heading around Novaya Zemlya, two large islands in the Arctic Ocean off the coast of Russia. But this trip didn't lead him to the Pacific either. The ship again hit crushing ice. It was all they could do to keep the ship from being pierced in the hull and sinking. Though some of the crew swore they saw mermaids during the miserable trip, the passage to the East was nowhere in sight.

And that's when Hudson made a secret decision. He thought he might reach Asia if he sailed west toward North America, so why not try that route now? He didn't have to tell the crew. He'd just steer the ship in that direction, and when they found the Pacific, they'd all be happy with the result. The weather and conditions would probably be better that way, anyway.

Hudson began to head west, but the misery continued. More ice. More danger. More rough seas — and no passage to the East anywhere. Soon the crew, led by Juet, discovered that their captain had duped them. They were furious. They insisted he return to England.

When a crew is insubordinate, the captain is free to jail them and bring them to trial, but Hudson did none of that. He agreed to the crew's terms. After lying to them and going against his contract with the Muscovy Company, maybe he thought he had no choice. And maybe he was right.

Hudson knew the Muscovy Company would be annoyed that he hadn't fulfilled their hopes of a northern sea route to the East. He was right about that too. They were not pleased with his lack of results. They told him they weren't funding any more of his voyages. Henry Hudson was fired.

Hudson fell into a depression. He felt like a loser and a failure. His friends tried to cheer him up and told him he was a great explorer, but he didn't believe it. Nothing helped until the Dutch came calling.

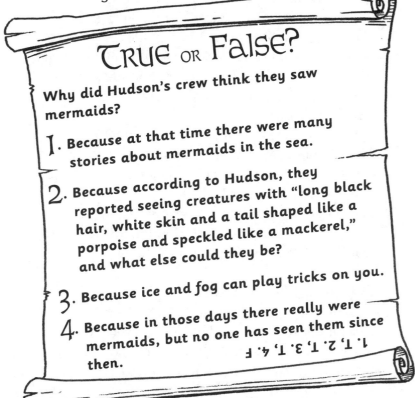

TRUE OR False?

Why did Hudson's crew think they saw mermaids?

1. Because at that time there were many stories about mermaids in the sea.

2. Because according to Hudson, they reported seeing creatures with "long black hair, white skin and a tail shaped like a porpoise and speckled like a mackerel," and what else could they be?

3. Because ice and fog can play tricks on you.

4. Because in those days there really were mermaids, but no one has seen them since then.

1. T, 2. T, 3. T, 4. F

Henry Meets the Dutch

The Netherlands (another name for Holland) had recently achieved independence from Spain, which had ruled over them for years. The Dutch were now ready to make a splash with their own ventures — and one of those was trading and sailing. One of the richest of the Dutch trading companies, the Dutch East Indies Company, already had power, their own large fleet and the ability to make war and establish colonies. They were keen to find the northerly route to the spice lands of the East.

They heard about Hudson, his exploits and his joblessness, and they made him an offer. But they'd also heard that he changed course without permission, so they insisted he sign a contract that he'd stick to their agreed-upon route via the north and around Novaya Zemlya.

Hudson agreed to their terms, and the Dutch East Indies Company gave him a small ship called the *Half Moon*. His crew were half English and half Dutch (Hudson couldn't speak Dutch). And guess who else came along? Hudson's rival and enemy, Juet! It was a motley crew, but what could Hudson do? He had to explore and, besides, he needed the money.

Half Moon Headaches

The *Half Moon* set sail on April 6, 1609, and immediately the crew argued. They bickered over food. The English wanted pickled beef and the Dutch preferred pickled fish. They also argued over work duties. And the Dutch crew hated the endless cold and stomach-churning seas. They were used to warmer climates. This cold was too much!

They grumbled and they groaned, and Hudson decided they all needed to sit down for a heart-to-heart talk. Despite his signed contract with the Dutch East Indies Company, Hudson convinced the crew that their best bet was to head for North America. The weather would surely be better, and that was the way to the East anyway.

The crew agreed, and the *Half Moon* sailed for what is now Maine and explored along the east coast of North America. Soon they reached a wonderful wide river, which we now call the Hudson River.

Hudson continued to sail into what is now New York City, and he claimed the land for the Dutch. He also met local tribes, trading peacefully with some and getting into skirmishes with others. In one encounter, one of his crew was killed.

But Hudson sailed on, hopeful that he'd finally find his way to the East via the great river. But soon the river grew shallow. It was clear that deep as it was in spots, this river was getting him nowhere. He also knew that the Dutch were going to be furious with him for disregarding their agreement and still finding nothing.

Hudson headed back, but not to the Netherlands. He anchored in Dartmouth, England, for the winter. They'd rest there and he'd write to the Dutch and explain why he hadn't stuck to his contract. Surely they'd understand.

They didn't. The Dutch East Indies Company had had enough of Henry Hudson and his explanations

Voyages of the *Half Moon* and *Discovery*

and, to make matters worse, King James of England had Hudson arrested for working for a foreign power.

Henry Hudson protested. It wasn't fair. Everyone knew that explorers often sailed for foreign powers. King James finally calmed down, especially when his son supported Hudson. The prince liked Hudson so much that he even helped him acquire a new ship. Hudson was ready to explore again.

The Sad End

On April 17, 1610, Hudson and a crew of 22 men, including you-know-who — yes, Juet again! — and Hudson's son John, sailed off from London on a ship called the *Discovery*. This time Hudson was *encouraged* by his employers to find the route he wanted to travel to Asia — via the northwest.

But his joy was short-lived. The ship sailed smack into a storm off Iceland, and fighting broke out among the crew. Hudson took sides, and soon Juet was talking mutiny again.

They were finally able to sail free of Iceland in June and head west past Greenland. On June 25th they reached the Furious Overfall (now called Hudson Strait), north of modern-day Quebec, and torrents of water spun the ship through dense fog. It was scary and miserable, but it got worse when ice cut off their passage. More anger erupted in the crew. They wanted to head out of the misery and toward home, but Hudson convinced them to sail on.

In August they entered what we now call Hudson

Bay. Hudson was hopeful that this "great and whirling sea" was his long dreamed-of passage to Asia. They sailed south from Hudson Bay to James Bay (bounded by present-day Ontario and Quebec) and spent weeks looking for a way out, but they got nowhere.

By September the crew, led by Juet, moaned that they were doomed and that Hudson didn't know where he was going,

It was true, but Hudson was outraged. After all, he was still the captain. How dare they speak to him this way?

This time he was determined to stand up to Juet. And he did. He demoted him and the other disloyal members of the crew. Hudson's actions split the crew. Some opposed him. Some supported him.

But by now there were other, more pressing worries. It was late October and winter was coming. They had to wait out the winter stuck on a barren piece of land at James Bay with little food. Some men developed scurvy, which made their teeth rot and fall out. Others were reduced to eating moss and frogs. They barely survived to the spring and, although conditions improved with better weather, nobody was happy.

In June 1611, after being stranded for months, the *Discovery* was finally ready to sail again. Hudson was keen to keep looking for the Northwest Passage. His crew were sick and tired of the whole expedition and wanted to head home.

On June 21 a dispute rose over some missing

bread. Hudson was sure some of the men were hoarding food. Some of the crew were so insulted that Hudson would search their personal belongings and so furious at the misery of the whole expedition that they hatched a secret, mutinous plot to seize the ship and head home.

By dawn the next day, three crewmen pounced on Hudson and bound him, along with his son John and six other sailors, many of whom were sick. They dumped them into a small boat called a shallop. The ship's carpenter, Philip Straffe, wasn't forced into the shallop, but he loyally insisted on going with his captain. Then the boat was set adrift. Hudson and the nine men with him were never seen again.

What Happened to the Mutineers?

The 13 men who remained on the *Discovery* after the mutiny had a horrible trip back to England. Juet died of starvation. Other mutineers, like Henry Greene, were killed by Inuit when they went ashore for provisions. Only eight made it home alive.

It took about five years for the rest of the mutineers to be brought to trial. They blamed everything on Juet and Greene. They claimed that none of the mutiny was their fault. They said they didn't even know about it until it was happening, and some even said that Hudson left the *Discovery* on his own.

The court was in a quandary. Who knew what? Who did what? And what was Hudson's role in this entire debacle? In the end, the court let the eight men go free. The reason? It wasn't murder since Hudson and the men with him in the shallop were cast off within sight of inhabited land.

What Do We Think of Henry Hudson Today?

What did Hudson accomplish after all the disastrous trips, the endless misery and what seemed like dead ends? Much more than he imagined.

He sailed farther north than anyone had before and mapped the new places he explored. Because of his voyage, the Dutch claimed New York, the city on that mighty river that Hudson explored, although the Dutch didn't keep New York for long.

Hudson's explorations also led to England's claim

of the land around Hudson Bay and to the formation of the powerful Hudson's Bay Company.

Henry Hudson dared to go where no man had gone before. He thought that he'd discovered nothing special, but he was wrong.

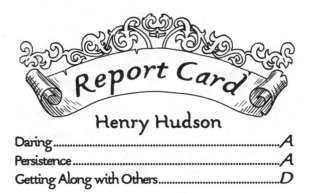

Report Card

Henry Hudson

Daring...A

Persistence...A

Getting Along with Others..D

Man on the Move

Captain James Cook (1728–1779)

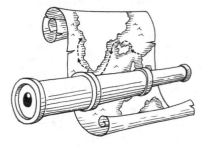

 What do you do if your ship strikes coral in the Australian Great Barrier Reef and gets a hole in its hull?

1. Dump stuff to lighten the ship.
2. Plug the hole with gum.
3. Plug the hole with dung.
4. Jump off the ship and swim with the sharks.

If you picked answers 1 or 3, you're right. In June 1770, Captain James Cook's ship, the *Endeavour*, hit jagged coral on the Great Barrier Reef. The crew tossed guns and even cannons overboard to lighten the ship. Then they patched the hole with a sail rolled in waterproof wool and dung. Voila! It worked.

Captain Cook, who is often called the greatest explorer of the 18th century, had to deal with many tricky situations in his three long voyages. Each new place he reached brought new challenges and new surprises. And not all the surprises were fun.

But James Cook was cool in a crisis. He was also a brilliant map-maker and savvy navigator who rose from a modest family to the highest rank in the English navy.

How did he do it? And why, after such an amazing career, was he murdered in Hawaii at the age of 51?

Who was James Cook?

James Cook was born into a large family in Yorkshire, England, on October 27, 1728. His father was a migrant farm labourer who couldn't afford to send his son to a good school. But James was clever, and he learned how to read and write from a farmer's wife. Later he attended a small local school and showed skill at arithmetic.

His first job was in a grocery store as a clerk, but he didn't like the work. He longed to go to sea and see the world.

When he was 18, he had his chance. He was offered a position as an apprentice by a local shipowner, and he took it. For nine years, he sailed up and down the coast of England in rough seas on a fleet of collier ships, which carried coal. In his spare time, he studied mathematics and became a skilled navigator. He was so good at his work and so clever at navigating that he was eventually offered command of a collier, but he refused. He had his sights on another career and employer — the Royal Navy.

In 1755 he volunteered as a seaman, although the work was hard, the pay terrible, the discipline harsh and, at 27, he was one of the *oldest* new navy seamen.

But France and England were at war in Europe (The Seven Years' War) and in North America (The French and Indian War), and Cook counted on moving up in the navy during wartime. How else could a man from a poor family make it BIG?

His bet paid off. Everyone was impressed with the tall, lanky young man's coolness, good nature and smarts. He rose in the ranks and was sent to Canada to help survey the St. Lawrence River and to take part in the English capture of Quebec.

For five summers he surveyed the Newfoundland coast and drew such accurate maps that they were used for many years. James Cook was definitely moving up!

Eat the Sauerkraut

In 1768, the navy had two important missions, and one was top secret. Who did they pick to lead it? A man of wealth and power? No! They picked an unusual choice for those times. Someone from a poor family who was skilful and cool under pressure — James Cook!

The official mission was to sail to Tahiti to observe the path of Venus across the sun, which would help scientists map the solar system. The secret mission was to search for *Terra Australis Incognita*, a giant southern continent that many in England were sure was lying somewhere in the south Pacific beyond Australia.

Cook asked for a collier and was given the

Endeavour to command. He'd sailed on many colliers and didn't mind that it wasn't a glamorous ship. All that mattered was that it was sturdy, reliable and could sail in shallow waters.

Cook insisted they reinforce its hull with horsehair and tar, and nail on thick planks so that the nasty, tropical sea worm wouldn't chew its way through the ship. Then the *Endeavour* would be fine for the journey. He wrote, "A better ship for such service I never would wish for."

They also filled the hold of the *Endeavour* with huge barrels of food and drink, six dozen hens, a goat, a pen full of pigs, surgeon's amputating knives (just in case), vinegar for scouring the decks, evaporated malt, fruit syrup, dried soups, and lots of sauerkraut. James Cook was one of the first to figure out that scurvy might be prevented if the crew ate the right food, like sauerkraut, even if they hated it!

They also crammed in enough hammocks for all the sailors in the crew. Many of them were as young as 12 years old. Only Cook and a few others were over 40.

A distinguished botanist named Joseph Banks joined the trip. Banks was wealthy and helped pay for the expedition. But Cook must have groaned as he watched Banks bring four servants, a naturalist, an astronomer, two artists and a secretary, plus boxes of specimen jars, books, easels, insect-catching equipment and two greyhound dogs onto a ship already overcrowded with men, animals and supplies.

Despite all the preparations, Cook's attention was

soon diverted from his missions when the expedition ran into problems. They lost an anchor on the island of Madeira, and the quartermaster drowned trying to retrieve it. In Rio de Janeiro, Brazil, a sailor fell off and drowned. In Tierra del Fuego, at the tip of South America, Joseph Banks hiked inland, got caught in a snowstorm, and two of his servants froze to death.

Finally they left the Atlantic, and headed for the Pacific. Hopefully their luck would improve in that ocean.

Mission Impossible?

Three weeks later they landed on lush, mountainous Tahiti. The crew of the *Endeavour* found it both gorgeous and strange. The Tahitian men and women were heavily tattooed. They stuck dyes into their skin with sharp rocks. During funerals, women beat their heads with shark teeth.

Despite its strangeness, Tahiti was so appealing that Cook had to haul a few of his sailors back on board who didn't want to leave the beautiful island and the friendly people who lived there.

While in Tahiti, Cook and his crew tried to fulfill Mission #1. They observed

the path Venus took. Unfortunately they couldn't see Venus clearly, so their calculations weren't accurate.

Mission #1 was sort of accomplished.

It was time for Mission #2 — finding the great southern continent that legend said was somewhere around in the Pacific. Cook sailed up, down and all over, but finally decided there was no continent anywhere he could see.

Mission #2 was accomplished — for now.

Turtles, Traitors and Kangurus (Kangaroos)

They next headed to New Zealand, where they encountered the fierce Maori people. They were so fierce they sometimes cannibalized their enemies. As Cook described it, the Maori had recently, "killed and eaten a boat's crew of their enemies."

At first Cook and his men clashed with the Maoris, but then they made peace by touching noses, which meant you were friends in Maori terms. Cook grew to admire the Maoris' skills as farmers, carpenters and carvers.

And while Cook charted the entire New Zealand coastline, Banks gathered plants.

The *Endeavour* sailed on to Australia (then called New Holland). They reached a spot where the sea was full of stingrays, and Cook called it Stingray Harbour. They later found so many unusual plants they called it Botany Bay, and Joseph Banks rushed around collecting plant samples no European had ever seen.

And then they hit the Great Barrier Reef, and

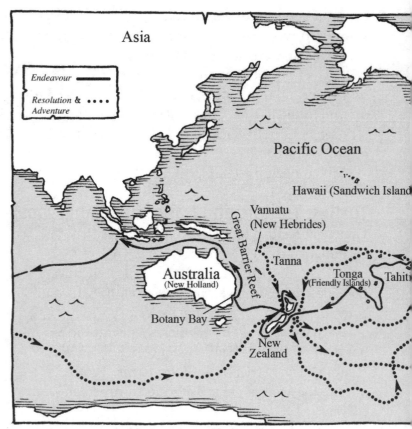

Voyages of the *Endeavour*, *Resolution* and *Adventure*

that's where the *Endeavour* almost sank. While the ship was being repaired, Cook marvelled at the giant sea turtles and the strange hopping creatures the locals called kanguru or kanguroos. They "resembled a wild dog but jumped up like a hare or a deer," Cook wrote.

It was all new and exciting, but it was almost three years since the *Endeavour* had left England. It was time

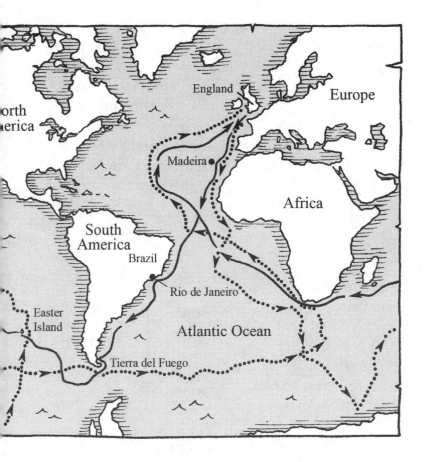

to head home. But on the way back, dysentery and malaria broke out, and only 56 men and one goat returned alive to England. The goat had survived not just one, but two voyages around the world. (He'd travelled earlier with explorer Samuel Wallis.)

Cook had charted 8,050 kilometres of coastline. He'd kept his crew almost free of scurvy through a good diet of fruit, vegetables and, of course, sauerkraut. Unfortunately other diseases killed many of the crew, but scurvy would have killed many more.

Cook was glad to be back and to see his wife and two older boys. Sadly his youngest son and his only daughter had died while he was away.

Cook was applauded back in England for his achievements, but not as much as Banks, who enjoyed showing off all his exotic plant specimens to an admiring public.

Brrrr...

The English government was now convinced that there was no southern continent near New Zealand and Australia, but what if Cook searched even farther south? What if he sailed to the very bottom of the world?

Cook agreed to continue searching for a southern continent. This time he took two colliers, *Resolution* and *Adventure*. He would travel with 110 naturalists and crewmen on the *Resolution*, while the *Adventure*, captained by Tobias Furneaux, would take 80 people along.

Botanist Joseph Banks would join the expedition

again. But this time Banks wanted to travel in real style. He planned to bring along more of his friends, more servants and even a horn player. He ordered special quarters to be built for his group.

Cook took one look at Bank's plans and said, "No!" The extra rooms would make the ship top-heavy and difficult to sail. Banks was furious. If he couldn't get his private quarters, he wasn't going. And he didn't.

Instead Cook took naturalist Johann Reinhold Forster and his son, Johann Georg, surveyor George Vancouver and artist William Hodges. He also took along a new and revolutionary piece of equipment, a chronometer, or sea clock, recently invented by John Harrison to measure longitude, which Cook soon called his "trusty watch."

On July 13, 1772, the two ships departed from Plymouth, England, heading to Cape Town, South Africa. Two weeks later they crossed the Antarctic Circle.

Cook soon discovered that the Antarctic was an even tougher place than the Arctic, where explorers like Hudson had ventured. Unlike the Arctic, there were few edible animals and no local people in the Antarctic — just mountains of ice.

It was terrifying and thrilling to see such huge icebergs. It was just plain terrifying to be tossed by violent winds over gigantic waves in freezing seas. And then there was fog so thick that the *Resolution* couldn't see the *Adventure*, and the two ships were separated.

After sailing on, Cook had no choice but to leave the frozen Antarctic and turn east toward New Zealand.

There he met up with the *Adventure* and gathered provisions.

The Beautiful, the Weird and the Creepy

Cook now decided to head away from the endless ice and explore more of the balmy South Pacific. He soon landed on the beautiful islands of Tonga. Cook and his crew called them the Friendly Islands because of the warm welcome they received. Even so, they found some of the local people's customs strange — like when they lopped off the joints of some of their fingers to sacrifice to their gods.

And that wasn't the only odd place they visited. Easter Island was an isolated, barren land full of mysterious stone statues. And then there was the New Hebrides, with their unfriendly, stone-throwing people, and Tanna, where they watched an active volcano.

But worse than a spewing volcano was sailing south, encountering mountains of impenetrable ice again and again, then returning to New Zealand to discover that the *Adventure*, which had arrived before them, had sent ten of its crew to shore, where the men had been murdered. The captain of the *Adventure* was so devastated that he headed for home.

And soon so did James Cook and the *Resolution*. They arrived back in England on July 30, 1775, after a three-year voyage covering over 96,000 kilometers (60,000 miles). It had been a harrowing, eye-popping, endlessly surprising trip. And luckily, despite the cold, some unfriendly locals and diseases, most of the people on the *Resolution* had made it back alive!

Cook was also now certain that there was no habitable southern continent. There was just ice. And that was that!

The Beginning of the End

On Cook's return to England, he was lauded as a great seaman, navigator and explorer — especially since none of his sailors had died of scurvy.

Now the Earl of Sandwich encouraged Cook to go on another voyage. The English were still desperate

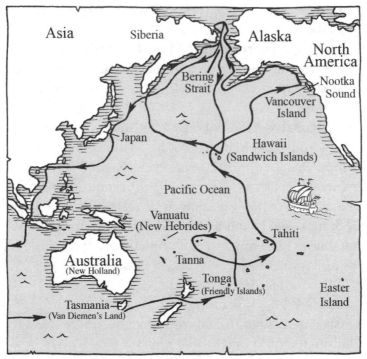

Cook's last voyage aboard the *Resolution*

to know if there was a Northwest Passage to the riches of the East. Maybe they could get to it from the Pacific Ocean. They were so keen; they even offered a hefty cash reward to anyone who could achieve that feat. The Earl thought James Cook was just the man for the job.

You'd think James Cook would have had enough of exploring by now. You'd think he'd want to stay home and enjoy his fame and family. But he was restless and he yearned to explore again.

On July 12, 1776, Cook and the *Resolution* left Plymouth. The ship carried people and lots of animals like cattle, pigs, sheep, cats, dogs and rabbits. Cook called it "a Noah's Ark."

At Cape Town, South Africa, the *Resolution* was joined by the *Discovery*, led by Captain Charles Clerke, and off they sailed to try to find the elusive Northwest Passage.

But as this trip went on, something was different about James Cook. Instead of his usual calm, cool temper, he got angry. He was even cruel. Was it too many years at sea, or was he ill with some kind of infection? We'll never know for sure. What we do know is that on one island he burned down a house while searching for a missing goat, and on another island he had a thief's hair and ears cut off.

Then after almost two years at sea, in late January 1778, Cook and his ships came upon three unsheltered, beautiful volcanic islands, where women danced the hula and people rode the waves on a wide plank of wood. (He landed in what we now call

Hawaii.) The local people thought Cook was their returning god, and he called this place the Sandwich Islands.

After his visit to the lush Sandwich Islands, Cook sailed on to Nootka Sound on what is now Vancouver Island. Cook and his men were thrilled to trade items like nails for the local sea otter fur. Cook raved in his journal about the softness of the otters' fur. (After his

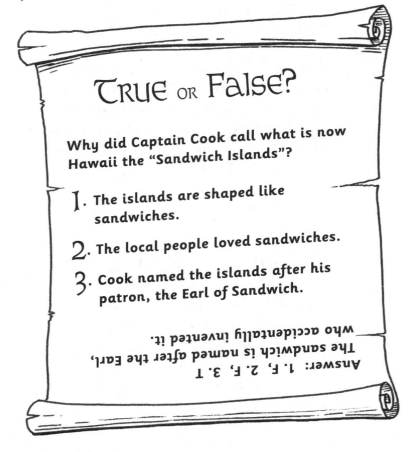

TRUE OR False?

Why did Captain Cook call what is now Hawaii the "Sandwich Islands"?

1. The islands are shaped like sandwiches.

2. The local people loved sandwiches.

3. Cook named the islands after his patron, the Earl of Sandwich.

Answer: 1. F, 2. F, 3. T
The sandwich is named after the Earl, who accidentally invented it.

expedition so many traders came, and so many sea otters were killed for their fur, they almost became extinct.)

After Nootka Sound, Cook sailed through the Bering Strait, which separates Siberia from Alaska. From there, Cook steered his ships through dense fog and walls of ice. For four months they drifted through the barren icy Arctic Sea, but they couldn't find a passage anywhere. It wasn't till they were almost trapped in the ice that Cook knew he had to head south.

Cook returned to the Sandwich Islands to repair his battered ships. And that's when everything fell apart. The Hawaiians stole a large cutter (a rowboat) from the *Discovery*. Cook was furious and confronted them. Fighting broke out, and the Hawaiians killed Captain Cook on the shore of Kealakekua Bay, on what is now the Big Island of Hawaii.

How sad that such a great captain and explorer died so violently in such a beautiful place.

What Do We Think of Cook Today?

James Cook was a brilliant navigator, map-maker and captain. He was the first European to map the East Coast of Australia. He kept his men fairly free of scurvy and used new navigational instruments like the chronometer. He sailed close to Antarctica but never stepped on that frozen southern continent.

He added hugely to Europe's knowledge of the Pacific, but he also inadvertently brought dreadful diseases to many of the people in lands he and his crew visited.

James Cook had longed "not only to go farther than anyone had before but as far as possible for man to go."

He did exactly that.

Report Card

James Cook

Daring.. *A*

Persistence..*A*

Getting Along with Others.....................................*B*

Road Buddies

Meriwether Lewis (1774–1809)
And William Clark (1770–1838)

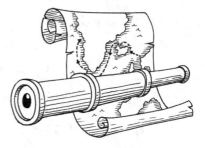

 What do you do if you're president of the
United States and you've convinced the
US Congress to buy a huge chunk of land?

1. Throw a party to celebrate.
2. Send other people out to explore the land,
   because you're too busy being president.
3. Send your personal secretary to explore.
4. Send your neighbour.

If you picked answer 2, 3 or 4, you're right. In
1803 President Thomas Jefferson of the United States
convinced Congress to buy the Louisiana Territory of
North America from Emperor Napoleon of France.
Jefferson had already asked his personal secretary and
neighbour, Meriwether Lewis, to lead an expedition to
explore the West. This new purchase made the timing
for that journey perfect.

Although Lewis was excited to explore, he knew it

was too big a job for one person. He needed someone smart, steady and savvy, so he asked his former army commander, William Clark, to co-captain the expedition.

About 31 men, dubbed the Corps of Discovery, including carpenters, hunters and tailors, and a Newfoundland dog called Seaman, would come along too. One woman, Sacagawea, would join them, and she would become crucial to the success of the journey.

How did the members of the Corps get along, despite treacherous roads, tough times and dangerous terrain? What surprising places did they see, and what strange experiences did they have on this amazing expedition?

Who Was Meriwether Lewis?

Although the name Meriwether means someone who has a sunny disposition, that word didn't match Meriwether Lewis's personality. He was fair-minded, brave, intelligent — and moody. He was born in Virginia in 1774 and raised on a large plantation. He liked plants and learned about them from his mother, who was an expert on herbs.

He joined the army in 1794 and served on the frontier for six years. He then served as personal secretary to President Jefferson. Even though he was only 29 years old, the president trusted him with the mission to explore the west and see, if there was a water route all the way to the Pacific. Jefferson wrote: "Capt. Lewis is brave, prudent, habituated to the woods and familiar with Indian manners and characters. He is not regularly educated but he possesses a great mass of accurate observation on all the subjects of nature which present themselves here . . . ."

It was good that Jefferson trusted Lewis, because it was going to be tricky exploring territory that didn't belong to the United States — yet. Over the years the land had flip-flopped between Spain and France, and now was under French control.

How would the French feel about a bunch of American explorers tramping through their land, asking questions and mapping rivers and mountains? Emperor Napoleon of France wasn't an easy fellow to deal with at the best of times. He was hungry for power and ruthless in the pursuit of it. He'd marched across Europe conquering everything and everyone in his path.

So Jefferson decided to ask Napoleon to sell him the port of New Orleans. At least that way, the United States would have access to one important slice of the Louisiana Territories. But the French wouldn't sell.

Let's Make a Deal

Soon after Jefferson's request, France and England were ready to go to war, and Napoleon had a change of heart. He needed money to fight the British. He also figured that since France was far away from the territory and the United States was so close, the Americans might eventually overrun the land anyway. Why not sell now?

The Louisiana Purchase

Napoleon offered to sell the entire Louisiana Territory (more than two million square kilometres, or more than 800,000 square miles, stretching from the Gulf of Mexico to Canada and from the Mississippi River to the Rocky Mountains) to the United States for just 15 million dollars. What a deal!

Jefferson was stunned and delighted. And although some people in Congress thought the purchase was a waste of money, Jefferson cajoled Congress into buying it anyway.

Now Lewis could explore land that belonged to America, not France. (In those days, the United States didn't worry too much about the Native peoples' rights to the land. They viewed them as just a thorny problem to be handled.)

Lewis immediately began studying maps, plants and navigation, and buying scientific instruments. He also realized he couldn't lead this expedition without help. But who could he ask to join him on such a huge and risky adventure? It had to be someone he trusted. Someone who was calm, smart, knew mapping and could handle tough days of exploring.

The first person he thought of was William Clark. Clark was a few years older than Lewis. In June 1803, Lewis wrote to Clark, "There's no man on earth with whom I should feel equal pleasure in sharing . . . as with you." Lewis asked Clark to be co-captain of the expedition.

But then Lewis didn't hear back from Clark. He waited and waited and, by late July, Lewis decided to ask someone else. But before he could, he got a letter from Clark. Clark had written back immediately, but the mail was slow.

POP QUIZ What would you do if your friend asked you to explore a land that might be full of giant beavers, prehistoric mastodons and unicorns?

1. Tell him, "No way!"
2. Tell him, "Of course! I've always wanted to see terrifying and weird creatures like giant beavers, mastodons and unicorns."
3. Tell him you'd love to explore dangerous and uncharted new places with him.

If you picked answer 3, you're right. Clark was delighted to join his friend and head into the unknown.

Who Was William Clark?

William Clark was born on a plantation in Virginia on August 1, 1770. His five older brothers had all served in the American Revolution, and one of them had become a hero in defeating the British out West.

The West would always be part of Clark's life. His family even moved westward to Kentucky when Clark was 14.

In his 20s, Clark served as an officer in the United States army but resigned in 1796 to manage the family's plantation.

Unlike Lewis, William Clark was tall, calm and jovial. Despite their differing temperaments, the men trusted each other and divided the responsibilities fairly between them. Lewis was in charge of measuring distances and collecting plants and minerals. Clark was in charge of maps and meals. They'd both keep journals. And sometimes they'd switch jobs if necessary.

In the fall of 1803, Lewis travelled by keelboat down the Ohio River to Louisville, Kentucky, where he picked up Clark. They made preparations and set up their first winter camp in mid-December on the Mississippi River near the village of St. Louis. All winter they organized their expedition. They knew they needed three things to succeed: enough food, good relations within the Corps of Discovery and with the Native peoples they'd encounter along the way, and a lot of luck.

After all, they were heading into unknown territory and who knew what dangers lay ahead. It didn't take long for the Corps to discover that this trip was going to be dangerous and grueling.

By late spring, they headed up the Missouri River, towing a big keelboat and two smaller boats against the current. The men were forced to stand knee-deep in water and mud while dragging the boats upstream. Everyone had to be careful. If someone hit a jagged dead tree under water, it might rip a hole right through a boat.

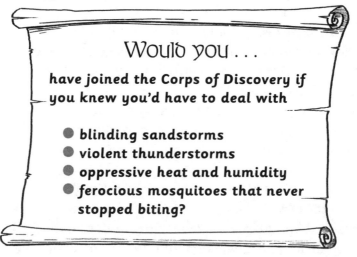

Would you . . .

have joined the Corps of Discovery if you knew you'd have to deal with

- **blinding sandstorms**
- **violent thunderstorms**
- **oppressive heat and humidity**
- **ferocious mosquitoes that never stopped biting?**

And that was just the beginning of their troubles. The Corps ran into miserable weather, vicious bugs, unexpected illness and accidents. In August a member of the Corps, Sergeant Charles Floyd, died of a ruptured appendix. (Given the dangers of their expedition, it's amazing that he was the only member of the group to die on the entire journey.)

In September, Clark noticed the sandbar they were camping on was collapsing. He acted quickly and no one drowned.

On another day, Lewis slipped off some sandstone cliffs while he and Clark were climbing up to carve their names. "He saved himself by the assistance of his knife," Clark wrote.

By October they reached the Hidatsa and then the Mandan villages along the river, in what is now North Dakota. They decided to stay in this area for the second winter, with the Mandans permitting the building of Fort Mandan. And that's where they met Sacagawea.

Sacagawea! We Couldn't Have Made It Without You!

The Mandans gave the Corps members food, protection and information, but their best help came in the form of Sacagawea, a 16-year-old Shoshone woman.

Sacagawea had been kidnapped when she was about 12 by a war party of Hidatsas, who were enemies of the Shoshone. At some point, another young Shoshone woman, as well as Sacagawea, had become the wives of Toussaint Charbonneau, an older, French-Canadian fur trader. Shortly after Lewis and Clark arrived, Sacagawea gave birth to a son called Jean Baptiste. Her husband was hired as an interpreter, and with him, she and the baby boy joined the Lewis and Clark expedition.

Sacagawea spoke the Hidatsa and Shoshone languages and helped interpret for the Corps. Her presence reassured the local tribes that the Corps was coming in peace. She also knew how to gather edible berries, roots and nuts when food was scarce. The expedition needed all the expert help they could get to survive, as they headed into unknown lands and unknowable dangers.

After leaving Fort Mandan in the spring of 1805, the Corps dragged their boats against the Missouri current and through the rugged prairie land. They were lucky to have Sacagawea along, especially when the boat she was riding in almost capsized in the wind. She held onto important supplies and papers, and they didn't fall overboard. Despite the danger, she stayed cool and calm.

But soon she would help Lewis and Clark in an even more crucial way. They'd soon have to climb steep mountains, and they needed horses to make the difficult trek.

The Lucky/Unlucky Corps

Luckily, they were close to Shoshone land, and the Shoshones had horses. In August when the group neared Sacagawea's tribe and arranged to speak to the chief, Sacagawea realized that it was her long-lost brother Cameahwait. She was overjoyed to see him again. She asked the Shoshones to sell horses to the Corps. And they did.

The Corps began to climb the Rockies. Luckily, they now had animals that could climb up the treacherous, narrow trails. Unluckily, they ran out of food in freezing conditions in the Bitterroot Mountains,  which a member of the Corps called "the most terrible mountains I have ever beheld," and they had to eat some of those horses.

Luckily, they encountered the Nez Perce people, who gave them some dried salmon and pounded roots. Unluckily, the unfamiliar food made them violently ill. Luckily, with the kindness and attention of the Nez Perce, they survived.

That wasn't the end of their troubles. There were unpleasant surprises waiting at every bend in the road, and over every hill and mountain pass. As they crossed rapids, portaged over rocks, navigated high waterfalls and steep canyons, they lost canoes and supplies. The days were long, hard and miserable.

But finally they were nearing the coast. Finally they were close to the Pacific Ocean! Maybe the journey would be easier now.

It was the first time any of the Corps had seen this vast, beautiful ocean. Clark wrote: "Ocian in view. O! The joy!" (As you can see from the way Clark spelled "ocean," spelling was not his best subject. He also spelled mosquitoes in 19 different ways in his journal.)

Rain! Rain! And More Rain!

Their joy was short-lived.

The west coast was wet. It rained all the time. They paddled in damp clothes, dodged huge, fast-floating tree limbs that almost crashed into their canoes and stones cascading from the hills and mountains. They had little food except the awful dried fish, and the local tribes had a habit of stealing their stuff. They were wet and annoyed.

They were also stuck. They had to stay on the rain-drenched coast for the winter. They made camp near present-day Astoria, Oregon.

The rain kept coming and the misery never stopped. Luckily, the men in the Corps were able to

make some new clothes from tanned elk, since most of their old clothes had rotted right through from the rain and damp.

One day they heard about a stranded whale, and they all rushed down to the beach. They were so hungry; a little whale blubber was just the thing to perk them up. Sacagawea raced to the beach too. She'd never seen a whale.

By the time they reached the shore, the local tribes had reduced the whale to a skeleton, but at least the Corps was able to buy a little blubber and some whale oil.

Heading Home Isn't Easy Either

Spring finally came.

In April the Corps was ready to head back east. They knew that going back wasn't going to be easy. They had to face the same difficult conditions they'd encountered on the way west.

And they were right. The rapids were just as wild as before, and the food was just as scarce. The mosquitoes were just as vicious — some men even inhaled some. Once they had to barter their buttons for food. Luckily Clark, who knew about medicine, though he wasn't officially a doctor, helped some local tribes and was rewarded with a horse. But the Corps was so hungry they ate the horse.

In early July, after they had crossed the Bitterroot Mountains, Lewis decided it would be a good idea if they divided the Corps into smaller groups. He'd explore the Northern Missouri near Canada, and Clark would check out the Yellowstone River. Then they'd meet up again.

It was a bad idea. Lewis and his group got into a skirmish with some Blackfoot warriors, and a few Blackfoot tribesmen were killed. It was the most violent episode of the whole two-year journey.

Ouch!

Soon after, while hunting near the Yellowstone River, one of the men in the Corps mistook Lewis for an elk and shot Lewis in the rear. Lewis was in agony. Sitting was excruciating.

When the Corps finally reached Fort Mandan, they paid Sacagawea's husband and said goodbye to Sacagawea, whose wise counsel and kindness had

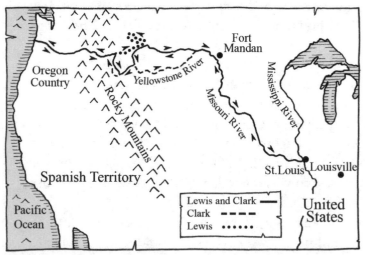

Lewis and Clark expedition

helped them through many dangerous situations. She'd never complained, but trekked on, despite having a young son to care for throughout the long, arduous journey.

The Corps finally reached St. Louis to a joyous welcome and celebration on September 23, 1806.

A Sad End for Meriwether Lewis

At first Lewis enjoyed his fame and the money he made from the expedition. He liked being named governor of the Upper Louisiana Territory. But he began to drink heavily, and his marriage proposal to a young woman was turned down. He became so unhappy that he didn't show up for a year to take the job of governor. Things just went from bad to worse. His moodiness turned into depression. In 1809, on his way to explain himself to the US government in Washington, he stopped at a backcountry inn in Tennessee. There he died of two gunshot wounds, probably self-inflicted.

A Busy Life for William Clark

Clark spent much of his life after the expedition working in Indian relations. He failed in a bid for governor of Missouri in 1820, so he continued working as a Superintendent of Indian Affairs. He had a reputation with everyone as a fair-minded man. He died in 1838.

A Short Life for Sacagawea

Six years after the expedition, Sacagawea gave birth to a daughter, Lisette. But soon after that, it is believed that she died of diphtheria at Fort Manuel, a Missouri Fur Company trading post in North Dakota.

Eight months after her death, William Clark became the legal guardian of her two children, Jean Baptiste and Lisette. Jean Baptiste was educated by Clark. It's not known if Lisette lived beyond infancy.

There have been rumours for years that Sacagawea didn't die at the age of 25, but lived on. What is certain is that although she was never paid for her work on the Lewis and Clark expedition, she was much appreciated for her wisdom and help, especially by William Clark.

What Do We Think of Lewis and Clark Today?

The members of the Lewis and Clark expedition brought back amazing specimens of plants and minerals, and records of the geography of the land they travelled. And they discovered that there was no straightforward water route all the way to the Pacific.

They also proved there were no unicorns, mastodons, or giant beavers (though there were lots of regular beavers) in North America. They dispelled many myths like these.

The Corps's detailed survey and maps helped America lay claim to the west and inspired many others to follow.

As for Sacagawea — she has more statues built in her honour than any other woman in the United States, and her face is on the one-dollar US coin.

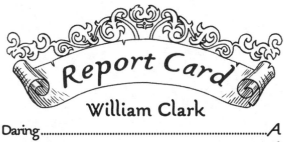

William Clark

Daring ....A
Persistence ....A
Getting Along with Others ....A

Meriwether Lewis

Daring ....A
Persistence ....A
Getting Along with Others ....B

Tragedy and Mystery
John Franklin (1786–1847)

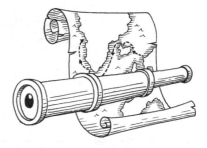

QUIZ Why do some people feel that explorer John Franklin was more famous in death than in life?

1. Because someone built a huge statue of him in London.
2. Because everyone wondered what happened to him and his crew in 1845.
3. Because at least 39 expeditions set out to discover the truth about his disappearance.
4. Because he had a holiday named after him.

If you picked answers 1, 2 or 3, you're right. English explorer Sir John Franklin, like many before and after him, set out to find the Northwest Passage. But his 1845 voyage to accomplish that ended in disaster. He and the crew of his two ships, the *Erebus* and the *Terror*, vanished. So did the ships.

His wife, Lady Jane Franklin, was so desperate to discover what happened to her husband and his expedition that she spent her fortune financing search parties. Because of Lady Franklin's relentless efforts and the public's curiosity to know what happened, pieces of the tragic tale have come to light over the years. In the end, the name of Franklin's ship, *Terror*, says it all. It is a story full of terror — starvation, disease, ice and probably cannibalism.

So who was this explorer who captained a risky expedition at the age of 59 — an age when many men in his day would have stayed home, read a good book or planted roses?

Who was John Franklin?

John Franklin was born in 1786 in Spilsby, Lincolnshire, England. His parents hoped he'd go into business or into the Church. But after a holiday on the coast, Franklin wanted to sail.

He persuaded his family to let him give the sea a try. As soon as he shipped out on his first voyage, he was hooked. In 1800 he took a job as a midshipman on board the *Polyphemus*. In 1801, while sailing on the *Investigator*, he took part in the brutal Battle of Copenhagen against the Danes.

After that, Franklin took off on more voyages and learned more about navigation and mapping. He even sailed to Australia with his cousin, Captain Matthew Flinders.

Everything was working out well for the young Franklin, until one of the ships he was sailing on crashed on an Australian coral reef in 1803. Franklin and the crew were stranded for over a month on a small island with few supplies. When he was rescued, he hopped on a ship home via China. He was 17 years old and had already been at sea for three years.

Franklin didn't stay long on land. He sailed on more ships and took part in more battles. He even fought in the war against French Emperor Napoleon. Although Franklin wasn't injured, the noise from the guns of those battles left him partially deaf for the rest of his life.

By 1808 he was promoted to lieutenant. In 1815, he took part in the Battle of New Orleans against the United States — a key battle that the English lost.

Despite the dangers, Franklin returned from it all in one piece. Now he was ready for something new. He'd become an explorer.

Find That Passage

For over 300 years the English were obsessed with finding the Northwest Passage that would link the Atlantic and the Pacific and be a shortcut to the East. The only trouble was all that annoying thick ice that blocked their way. Despite the ice, and all the failed expeditions like those led by Hudson and Cook, the English kept trying. Surely someone would discover a route through the ice. Surely the big cash reward they were offering would entice explorers to risk cold, ice, disease, starvation and maybe even death to find it.

Franklin was drawn to the challenge. He decided to join an Arctic expedition hoping to sail through the

Passage. He figured that even if they didn't succeed, he'd learn more about the conditions in the North. In 1818 he served as commander of a small ship, the *Trent*, under the orders of Captain Buchan, who was in charge of a bigger ship, *Dorothea*, and headed north.

But the ships didn't get through the ice. Like previous expeditions, the ice was so thick it almost crushed both ships. The badly damaged vessels limped back to England. The expedition was a failure, but Franklin was praised for his skills commanding the crew and his ship.

The word was out! There was a daring new explorer in England and his name was John Franklin.

Love That Explorer!

When Franklin returned from this first Arctic journey, he was delighted to meet a young poet named Eleanor Anne Porden. The two soon fell in love.

But before they could marry, Franklin told his bride-to-be that he had to attempt the Northwest Passage again. He was sure that this time it would be different. This time he'd be in charge. True, his expedition might be riskier than the ones before, because much of it would be overland, but Franklin was confident.

On this journey, they'd trek by foot, by canoe and venture into territory no European had seen before. Food for such a long, out-of-the-way journey was a concern, but they'd hire local people who'd help them with supplies. And they could hunt.

It would be tough, but it was worth a try! Imagine if they succeeded! The world, and especially their own countrymen, would cheer.

Bad Weather, Bad Food, Bad Trip

Starting out in the late summer of 1819, they'd head to the northwest coast of Canada, east of the Coppermine River. They hoped to find a route to guide them to the Northwest Passage.

Unfortunately, everything on the expedition went wrong.

By early autumn of 1821, they were in deep trouble. The canoes were difficult to manoeuvre in icy water. Food was scarce and there were few animals to hunt. The local guides didn't keep their word about helping out with supplies, and it was a bone-chilling winter.

Franklin pushed everyone as hard as he could, but

eventually even *he* had to admit defeat. They couldn't go on, or they'd all die. They had to return to base camp at Fort Enterprise.

But the trek back was gruelling too. All they had to eat was a bitter lichen called *tripe de roche*, or "rock guts." They even had to resort to eating the leather of their boots. It was all gross and hard to digest. Men began dropping of starvation or wandering off in confusion and never returning.

Franklin knew he had to make a decision and he had to make it fast. He decided that he and the men remaining would split up to reach help. Franklin and his small group trudged back, barely making it alive to the Fort. The other group bickered over food, and two men were shot dead in the dispute. Michel, one of the men shot dead, had even been suspected of eating one of his comrades.

The whole expedition had become a nightmare!

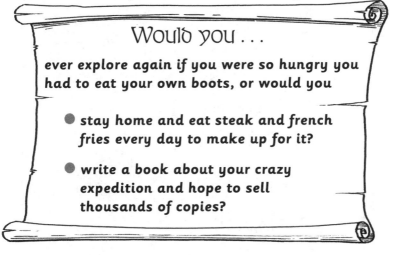

Would you . . .

ever explore again if you were so hungry you had to eat your own boots, or would you

● **stay home and eat steak and french fries every day to make up for it?**

● **write a book about your crazy expedition and hope to sell thousands of copies?**

All the remaining men, including John Franklin, were finally rescued and returned to England in 1822. And despite the horrific events and conditions, the expedition was applauded for charting new land. Franklin's book about his experiences, *Narrative of a Journey to the Shores of the Polar Sea in the Years 1819–1820,* became an instant bestseller despite its long title.

Franklin became known as "the man who ate his boots," but he didn't mind much; he was famous and

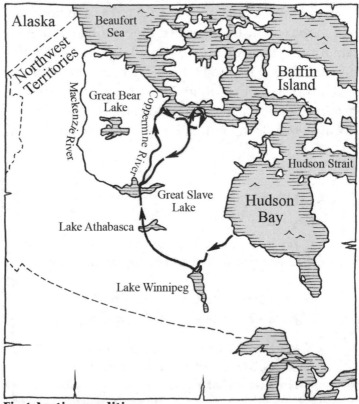

First Arctic expedition

a hero. He was also thrilled that he'd been promoted to captain in the Royal Navy. And despite all that he had endured, he was ready to set out for the Arctic again. But first he wanted to marry Eleanor.

Success and Sadness

John Franklin and Eleanor Porden were married in London in 1823. He was 37. She was 28.

A year later John and Eleanor had a daughter. But soon after the birth, Eleanor grew ill. She had tuberculosis and it had grown worse. In those days, there was no treatment.

Nevertheless, she insisted that her husband proceed with his plans for another expedition to the Arctic. She even gave him a silk Union Jack flag to stick into the Arctic ground.

When Eleanor recovered a little, Franklin decided it was time to plan his expedition. This time they'd take more food, more sensible clothing, sturdier boots and boats better suited to the icy conditions. Franklin also decided that the expedition would rely more on their own men than on local guides.

The expedition left England in 1825.

This time no one died on the journey. They mapped over 1,500 kilometers (930 miles) of coastline, made useful notes on the geology of the land and described the plants they found.

Their trip was a success! But Franklin's joy was mixed with heartbreak. When he reached his first outpost, he was informed that Eleanor had died one day after he had left England. At the farthest point of his expedition, full of sorrow, he planted her silk flag in the snow. He sailed back to England in 1827.

Second Arctic expedition

Life Gets Better

In 1828, Franklin married one of Eleanor's friends, Jane Griffin. He was knighted in 1829 and showered with awards and university degrees. He was now an esteemed explorer with a new wife.

In 1836 he took a completely new kind of job. He was appointed the Lieutenant-Governor of Van

Diemen's Land (now called Tasmania). As governor, he tried reforming the jail system and setting up schools and museums. The local people appreciated his efforts to make their lives better, but the politicians did not like his interference with their usual way of running the island. In 1843 he was recalled from his position.

How could he be fired? He'd worked so hard. And what was an ex-explorer and ex–lieutenant-governor to do now?

Explore again!

Too Old? No Way!

But wasn't Franklin too old, at 59, to face the hardships, the uncertainties and the misery of exploration?

Franklin didn't think so, and neither did the English government. Northwest Passage fever was heating up again. And although some people grumbled that Franklin was too old to lead a dangerous expedition, and some commented that he hadn't explored the Arctic in nearly 20 years, he took the job. He was raring to go!

This time he'd take two ships, *Erebus* and *Terror*, and they'd be well organized for the hardships they'd surely encounter. With a crew of 129 men, three years' worth of supplies (including a piano, good crystal, 1,200 books and lots of lemon juice to prevent scurvy) and reinforced steel ships with central heating and a good steam engine to plow through the ice, what could go wrong?

Sir Franklin, Make England Proud!

The two ships and their crew left England full of hope and confidence in May 1845. They were seen in late July off the coast of Baffin Island that year, and all was well.

But then the *Erebus* and *Terror* vanished.

No one worried for a while. It wasn't unusual in those days for ships to be out of touch. After all, they were off to places where mail couldn't be delivered. But by 1847, Franklin's family and friends began to worry. Why hadn't anyone seen or heard from Franklin's expedition in two years? Where were they? Were they still alive, or had something terrible happened?

Mrs. Franklin began to pester the government for answers. Go find my husband, she insisted. Find out where those ships are and what's happened to them. She even put up her entire fortune to discover her husband's fate.

A Mystery

Between 1847 and 1880, over 25 expeditions set out to find answers about the missing ships. After the 1880s, more expeditions set out. To this day, the mystery has perplexed, fascinated and confounded generations of scientists, researchers, historians, geographers and curious people everywhere.

This is what many now believe occurred. Thick ice and unrelenting freezing weather, the two elements that hampered or destroyed other expeditions to find the Northwest Passage, confronted the Franklin expedition too.

The investigators found a scribbled note left on a pile of rocks, written evidence that Franklin died on June 11, 1847, at the age of 61. By then his ships had been frozen in pack ice for nine miserable months. No one knows the exact cause of his death — just that it happened.

His second-in-command, Captain Crozier, had taken over the expedition. The two ships finally drifted south, but through more ice and wind. They drifted on and on, but got nowhere. They couldn't escape the ice or the weather. They were trapped. And more people soon died, many of disease.

Crozier figured they had no choice but to abandon the ships and try to make it back to safety over the ice. The remaining men trudged through the frozen wasteland and more of them died. Some even died of scurvy, despite all the lemon juice. Scientists now think it probably went bad. And some of them may have died of lead poisoning from the lining in the tins of the canned food. Others probably starved to death. There was evidence that some were so desperate they might have eaten their comrades. But no one knows for sure, because no one came back alive. And the remains of the ships have never been found.

The search expeditions have pieced together bits of evidence from tools, gravesites, skeletons and eyewitness reports, and have come up with different theories. All that's for certain is that the whole expedition was lost.

What Do We Think of Franklin Today?

Franklin was pretty close to navigating the Northwest Passage. He was brave, tenacious, generally decent to his men but not adequately prepared for the treacherous journey.

It would take another 70 years for an explorer to sail successfully through the Northwest Passage. His name was Roald Amundsen.

Report Card

John Franklin

Daring.. A
Persistence... A
Getting Along with Others.. A-

Last of the Vikings

Roald Amundsen (1872–1928)

After you've discovered the elusive Northwest Passage between the Atlantic and Pacific, what do you do next?

1. Retire to Florida.
2. Organize a parade to celebrate your achievement.
3. Check out some more icy places that no one has ever explored.

If you picked answer 3, you're right. Norwegian explorer Roald Amundsen successfully captained the *Gjøa* through the Northwest Passage between 1903 and 1906. It was a journey that many other explorers before him had attempted but failed, even though they had bigger ships and more men.

But sailing through the Northwest Passage was just the beginning for Amundsen. Why was this rugged Norwegian fascinated by frozen places no one had seen before, especially the North Pole? What made him flexible about changing plans? And how did he manage to get along with his colleagues, even though he was taciturn and liked to keep to himself?

Who Was Roald Amundsen?

Roald Engebreth Gravning Amundsen was born in Borge, Norway, in 1872. He grew up in a family of seamen and merchants, and read everything he could get his hands on about polar exploration. He devoured accounts of famous sea voyages like John Franklin's disastrous one in 1845. He was especially drawn to the hardships Franklin and his men endured. He wrote: "A strange ambition burned within me to endure those same sufferings."

He also studied and admired fellow Norwegian explorer Fridtjof Nansen's journeys criss-crossing Greenland in 1888.

From an early age, he decided to toughen himself up for polar exploration. He exercised regularly and kept his window open in the middle of icy Norwegian

winters to acclimate to frigid temperatures. He was determined to be physically and mentally ready to tackle the brutal conditions in polar exploration.

His parents weren't impressed with his exploring urge. They wanted him to become a doctor. Amundsen was a dutiful son, so he put his dreams aside and marched off to medical school.

But when his mother died when he was 21, he sold his medical books and shifted directions. Now he'd pursue his dreams of exploring the polar region, and he wasn't going to waste any more time.

He knew from studying past expeditions that you had be a skilled captain to be successful in tough, icy conditions. So, in 1894, Amundsen sailed aboard a sealing vessel to learn how to manage ships and sailors at sea.

Three years later, with that experience under his belt, he became first mate on the *Belgica*, a Belgian-financed ship heading for Antarctica and captained by explorer Adrien de Gerlache de Gomery.

Captain de Gerlache soon landed the ship in trouble. The *Belgica* froze in the ice and all aboard were isolated for 13 miserable months. Two sailors went mad and many fell sick with scurvy, including the captain.

Amundsen learned a lot about how to survive in icy conditions on this voyage, especially from his friend and fellow explorer Dr. Frederick Cook. When he finally returned to Norway, he was ready to lead an expedition himself.

You Can Always Count on the Dogs!

Amundsen decided that the first expedition he'd lead
would be to find the Northwest Passage between the
Atlantic and Pacific. It had eluded many explorers
before him, but he was sure he could find it. He also
figured he could get funding more easily if he attached
a scientific purpose to his expedition.

So he headed to Hamburg, Germany, and studied
magnetism, especially the magnetic north. Despite his
studies, he still had to use much of his own money,
and even go into deep debt, to fund a ship called the
Gjøa, a 30-year-old, 21-metre (70-foot) herring boat,
and man it with a crew of six. In June 1903 they sailed
for Greenland and then on to Baffin Island.

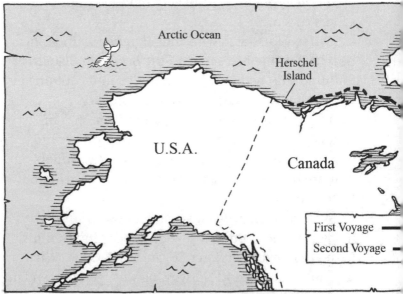

Search for the Northwest Passage aboard the *Gjøa*

Soon they encountered ice floes, fog, horrific winds and shallow water — all the conditions that had defeated other expeditions. But not Amundsen! His sturdy ship could handle shallow waters, and his skill kept them afloat and moving though the ice.

When the *Gjøa* arrived at King William Island, northwest of Hudson Bay, Amundsen decided to dock, build observatories and study the magnetic north. The crew made friends with the Inuit who lived in the area and were given gifts like fur underwear and caribou tongue.

They also learned more about living in freezing conditions. Soon they dressed like the Inuit and travelled on sleds pulled by dogs, as the Inuit did.

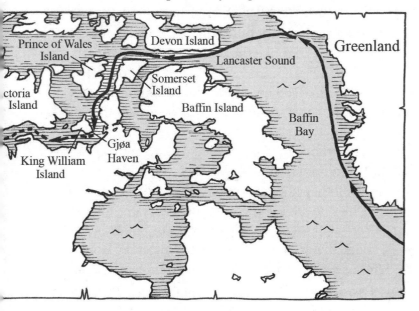

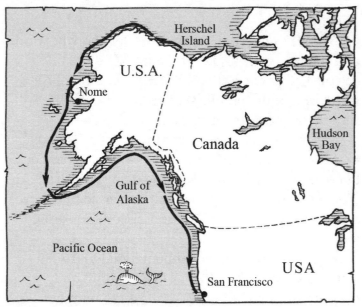

Passage through the Northwest

Amundsen realized that life was easier when you adapted to the cold like the locals, who were experts at it already.

In 1905 the *Gjøa* headed to the Alaska territory's south Pacific coast. Amundsen was confident that this was the way to the Northwest Passage — and he was right! They made it through the Passage on August 26th. What an accomplishment!

Now all they had to do was let the world know of his great achievement. But there was no telegraph station anywhere near them. The closest one was 800 kilometres (430 miles) away. How could Amundsen get the word out?

In one word — dogs. Amundsen had learned how valuable, trustworthy and hardy a pack of sled dogs could be, and he used them to mush all the way to the telegraph station and proclaim the news of his successful expedition through the Northwest Passage.

Everyone was impressed. He was now officially a famous Arctic explorer.

On to the North Pole!

Now what was Amundsen going to explore next? That was an easy question for a man who'd always been intrigued by the Arctic's North Pole. He'd go there, of course! He was ready. He was willing. He was going to achieve that too!

Since he was now a famous explorer, he figured he should be able to raise funds for his expedition. Luckily, famed Arctic explorer Nansen generously said he'd loan him his ship, *Fram*, for the journey.

All the pieces were falling into place.

And then Amundsen heard news that threw a wrench into all his plans: American Admiral Peary and Amundsen's friend Frederick Cook had reached the North Pole already. Oh no! Amundsen's dream shattered like an icicle knocked off a roof.

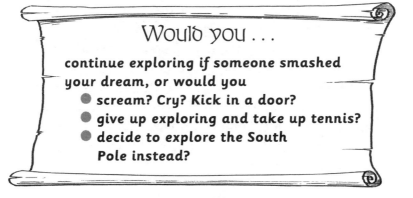

Would you . . .

continue exploring if someone smashed your dream, or would you
- **scream? Cry? Kick in a door?**
- **give up exploring and take up tennis?**
- **decide to explore the South Pole instead?**

Amundsen didn't shatter. No way! He'd find another dream and another frozen place to explore. Nothing was going to stop him. When he heard that Admiral Peary and Dr. Frederick Cook had reached the North Pole, he changed his plans.

Too Bad, Scott. I'm Heading South!

In 1909 Amundsen decided to shift his explorations from the North Pole to the South Pole and Antarctica. He studied what happened to Englishman Ernest Shackleton's attempt to reach the South Pole and how he failed only 157 kilometres (97 miles) from his goal.

He knew that Englishman Robert Scott was organizing his own second attempt to reach the South Pole. He also knew that the Norwegian government probably wouldn't endorse an Amundsen expedition, because they wouldn't want to upset the English. The press was full of news about Scott and his hopes to reach the South Pole.

Amundsen decided to keep his intentions secret. He didn't want anyone to scuttle his plans.

So what if he and Scott were trying for the same goal? He had a right to explore it too. And unlike Shackleton, he was going to take dogs and sleds. He called his dogs "our children," and said they "were the most important things for us." His experiences with the Inuit had taught him that these hardy dogs were comfortable with conditions on frozen land. They were tough and resilient. They'd pull Amundsen and his group to the South Pole.

While the whole world, including his crew, assumed Amundsen was headed north, Amundsen prepared to go south.

It wasn't till the *Fram* was out to sea that Amundsen spilled the beans to his crew. They were flabbergasted.

Amundsen sent Scott a telegram with the news of his change of direction. It read, "Beg leave to inform you *Fram* proceeding to Antarctic. Amundsen."

Of course Scott was shocked, but he stoically kept on with his mission. He too had studied Shackleton's trip, but he'd come to a different conclusion than Amundsen. Scott thought that Shackleton took all the right stuff — Siberian ponies, men and motorized sledges. Shackleton didn't take dogs, and neither would he. Dogs, he thought, would never be able to manage the long haul to the South Pole.

Of course, until now he hadn't thought this was a race. Still, his men were trained and ready to face whatever danger they'd encounter. He was sure of it.

They were Englishmen and proud of it. They couldn't let a sneaky Norwegian explorer like Amundsen win.

Who's First?

Scott's and Amundsen's groups both passed the winter of 1911 at different Antarctic bases. Then five men from each team set out for the South Pole.

Amundsen and his men set out on skis from a base closer to the Pole and 12 days earlier. They were lucky with the weather, the route and their dogs.

On December 14, 1911, the Amundsen team, with frost-bitten hands, proudly planted the flag of Norway in the South Pole ice. They later celebrated their achievement over seal meat and cigars.

Scott's ponies, on the other hand, weren't working out at all. The Scott team had to shoot them when they were still 580 kilometres (315 miles) from the Pole. The exhausted men, in terrible weather, then trekked on foot toward the Pole. When they finally neared it on January 18, 1912, they saw the Norwegians' tracks. What they'd feared had happened. Amundsen beat them to the Pole by more than a month!

Discouraged, they turned back, trudging through blinding snow and cold, with no dogs and little food. One by one, the men with Scott died of hypothermia and starvation. Scott was the last to die, in March 1912. He kept a journal to the end.

The bodies of Scott's party were found eight months later. They were only 18 kilometres (11 miles) from a food and fuel depot.

A Topsy-Turvy Victory

On March 7, 1912, Amundsen cabled his brother with the news that he'd reached the South Pole first. He was thrilled that he'd accomplished his goal, and yet, when he later wrote about his expedition, he noted: "I had better be honest and admit straight out that I have never known any man to be placed in such a diametrically opposite position to the goal of his desires . . . the North Pole itself had attracted me from childhood, and here I was at the South Pole. Can anything more topsy-turvy be imagined?"

To the world, Amundsen's journey seemed to have run smoothly and easily. He never received the credit for his ingenuity, tenacity and planning skills that one would expect.

Was it because he'd undertaken the expedition to the South Pole in secrecy? Was it because the English needed a hero like Scott, who was touted as brave and noble by his countrymen? Was it because it was sad that Scott's luck ran out and he'd been so close when he and his men died? Probably all of the above and more.

What's Left to Explore, Amundsen?

Amundsen had achieved so much already. He was the first man to navigate the Northwest Passage. He was the first man to reach the South Pole. What could he do now?

Return to his beloved Arctic again, of course. Explore it some more. Find something new. After all, he was always more drawn to the top of the world than to the bottom.

Amundsen tried to explore the Northwest Passage again, but this time by travelling a more northerly route. On this expedition, he didn't reach his goal. But he still wanted to keep exploring.

And that's when he became fascinated with flying.

In 1925 he made the first Arctic crossing in an airship designed by Umberto Nobile. Unfortunately, the two men had a falling-out. Despite that, when Nobile's plane, the *Italia*, crashed in the Arctic in 1928, Amundsen flew out to rescue him.

Nobile was rescued, but not by Amundsen. Three hours after Amundsen's plane took off, it disappeared. He was never seen or heard from again.

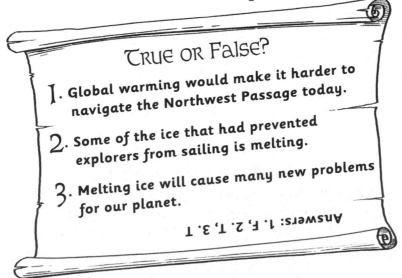

TRUE OR FALSE?

1. Global warming would make it harder to navigate the Northwest Passage today.

2. Some of the ice that had prevented explorers from sailing is melting.

3. Melting ice will cause many new problems for our planet.

Answers: 1. F, 2. T, 3. T

What Do We Think of Amundsen Today?

Roald Amundsen liked being called "the last of the Vikings." Like many Vikings, he was powerfully built and daring. But unlike them, he didn't want to maraud or to conquer anyone or anything, except icy lands that no one had explored before. And he did so with careful preparation, steady skill and respect for people like the Inuit, who knew how to survive in a tough environment.

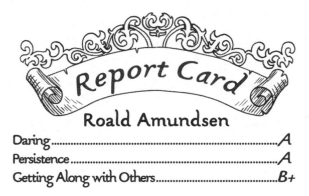

Report Card

Roald Amundsen

Daring..*A*

Persistence..*A*

Getting Along with Others...*B+*

What I've Leared About Explorers

1. You have to yearn to explore no matter what the consequences to your family, your health or your sanity.

2. You have to be tough, daring and tenacious.

All of the explorers in this book had those qualities in abundance. They were all driven to seek the unknown, despite unbelievable hardships, relentless misery and crushing disappointments.

Some, like Columbus and Hudson, never achieved their goals, although Columbus, to his dying day, thought he had.

Some, like Columbus and Cortés, were dismissed and discounted by their country after their last expedition.

A few, like Hudson, Cook and Franklin, died while exploring.

Many wrote eloquently about their expeditions in journals and books. And one, Marco Polo, was called a liar when he described his travels and adventures.

I also learned that explorers were influenced by reading and hearing about the explorers before them: Columbus was intrigued by Marco Polo's journey. Cortés was enthralled by Columbus's exploits.

Amundsen was fascinated by Franklin's expeditions.

They were all also influenced by the times in which they lived.

- There were few women explorers — because society discouraged women from exploring until the twentieth century.
- Cortes's cruelty to the people he conquered was not unusual for a Spanish conquistador of his times.
- Slavery was not new when Columbus enslaved Native peoples in the New World.

And yet, like each of us, an explorer's behaviour is also shaped by his temperament and personality.

- Eric the Red's temperament was more hotheaded and violent than his son Leif's.
- Champlain honoured his contracts, while Henry Hudson did not.
- Meriwether Lewis could be moody, while his expedition partner, William Clark, was usually jovial.

But despite different times, different personalities and different outcomes, each explorer transformed the world he lived in.

I wonder what each of them would think about the world today that they helped create.

F.W.

INDEX

Frieda Wishinsky says she has lost track of the number of children's books she has published: "Over forty, maybe fifty." They include picture books, non-fiction, novels and chapter books. Her non-fiction book *Everything But the Kitchen Sink,* co-authored with Elizabeth MacLeod, was winner of the Red Cedar Information Book Award and was named a Silver Birch Honour Book. Frieda lives with her husband in Toronto, Ontario.